EXECUTIVE

7 Easy Steps to a Proven
Strategic Operating System

Antoinette Braks

This book is dedicated to my parents with my wholehearted gratitude for their lifelong commitment, care and encouragement supporting me to realize my highest aspirations.

PREFACE

My Perspective

As a corporate gypsy who has traveled much of the world leading People and Culture in large and medium sized organizations, and coaching and consulting to Senior Executives in Strategic Leadership, Organizational and Leadership Development, I have found that our amazing potential to create and realize a vastly improved future is inhibited by the way our organizations operate.

Rather than releasing our capacity to achieve significantly improved outcomes and create a better world, they inhibit, constrain and limit us. Red tape, bureaucratic approval processes and a prevailing focus on risk management reduces our effectiveness and suspends our development. They rob us of our power to create.

Conventional organizational processes are the legacy of previous leaders who have reacted to the unethical behaviour of a few by seeking to limit decision-making as much as possible. While technology continues to enable us to streamline and automate work processes, our opportunity to realize our human potential is stifled.

This inhibits our evolution! It constitutes an urgent SOS call for help!!!

We were born to evolve, to develop our capacity to lead fulfilling, exciting lives and support and encourage all members of our community to do the same. We did not start out on our careers to live a humdrum existence in order to secure a pay check at the end of each week or month, notwithstanding how big that pay check is.

My Purpose

It has been my purpose in my life and career to enable people to realize their potential and organizations, their aspirations. As a result of this commitment, I have observed, participated in and learned how organizations operate. I have also studied human potential in terms of action orientation, emotional awareness, mindful attention, spiritual intelligence and neuroscience in relation to the development of our leadership capacity.

As a result I have experimented with new approaches to organizational transformation that have been remarkably successful albeit sometimes confronting to conventional managers. I then learned how to bring my colleagues and other stakeholders with me so that we could transform the organization as a whole. Through action learning I discovered how to transcend conventional operating systems with a more Strategic Operating System that enables us to tap into our unrealized potential.

In recent years I have taken my innovative approaches into my coaching conversations with more than 50 Senior Executive clients mostly leading divisions and organizations of between 100 and 1000 people. They were highly intelligent, capable and successful executives who wanted to become more inspiring, strategic leaders.

A Proven Solution

Through the course of multiple collaborative coaching sessions, I distilled the Seven Steps to establishing a Strategic Operating System. They all serve to unlock our creativity, more than double our productivity, empower our employees to make aligned decisions, engage multiple stakeholders to become active participants, lift our profile and aspirational voice in our community and generate breakthrough results.

These outcomes have manifested time and again with my executive clients. In my doctoral research study calibrating their leadership capacity before and after a 12-month coaching period, every single client shifted a full stage in leadership development. Most moved from *Achiever* to *Catalyst*, and two to *Strategist*. And they also realized aspirational goals and achieved breakthrough results

For me this not only proves the phenomenal value of the Strategic Operating System to uplift our lives and those of the people we lead and serve, but also the intransigence of current organizational practices that hold us back. We already have the latent leadership capacity to live into a much higher version of ourselves; we just need to operate more strategically to live into that potential.

Your Personal Journey

This book is for every Senior Executive who wants to advance and accelerate their career, set and realize higher aspirational outcomes and lead a more fulfilling life. The Seven Steps to establishing your own Strategic Operating System will enable you to break free of obsolete management practices and realize breakthrough results to create a better world.

Welcome! You will thoroughly enjoy your personal journey in self-evolution and the transformation of the organization you lead! While there will be challenges and concerns, new insights and opportunities will also emerge in at least equal number. And as you persist, you will be amazed by what transpires in your life. You will once again be excited as each new day dawns and you will also get balance and wellbeing back into your life.

In the following chapters you will find case studies of a selection of my clients who have lifted their careers to a higher octave in leadership alongside the accomplishment of transformational business outcomes. You will also discover and appreciate the shifts in paradigms, principles and practices that will increase your self-awareness of how you can elevate and expand your leadership capacity so you too can realize your true potential and the aspirations you hold for your organization.

All the very best,

Antoinette Braks

For more information on Stage Leadership Development, go to www.antoinettebraks/stages

For more information on Executive SOS, go to www.antoinettebraks/sos

Table of Contents

VOICE

STAGE LEADERSHIP

Alchemist

Strategist

Catalyst

Achiever

Specialist

Conformist

Opportunist

"The higher our self-expression and the deeper our self-awareness,
The richer our life experience and the greater our soul evolution."
- Antoinette Braks

Development Psychology

Stage Leadership is part of development psychology. It represents a progressive series of leadership capacities that reflect the development of new mindsets, world views or perspectives at progressively higher vantage points from which we see and interpret the world. It incorporates Einstein's view that: "You can't solve problems at the level they were created." We need to develop our leadership capacity to rise above the conventional world in order to generate transformational solutions. We need to be able to see the forest for the trees, or get onto the balcony of the dance floor, to "see" with a broader and deeper perspective.

The psychology of human development began with Abraham Maslow, the founder of humanistic developmental psychology. He focused on the means to achieving individual wellbeing and personal fulfilment in contrast to the overwhelming majority of psychologists at the time who were focused on the sources and symptoms of psychological dysfunction. Maslow preferred to give his attention to the aspirational lives led by some of society's most respected leaders. He created a Hierarchy of Needs portraying five sequential human needs that we each try to fulfil one at a time in order to increase our sense of wellbeing and fulfilment.

Maslow's Hierarchy of Needs incorporated:

1. Survival needs for air, water, food, rest, shelter and clothing

2. Security needs for physical safety, health, economic security and property

3. Belonging needs for family, friends, intimacy, colleagues and

community

4. Self-Esteem needs to feel confident, worthwhile and respected by others

5. Self-Actualizing needs to be authentic, creative and enjoy a purposeful and meaningful life.

Other researchers and practitioners in leadership development have since extended this list to calibrate levels of psychological human development within the frame of "Self-Actualizing" as shown in the table below. Maslow's five needs and the continuing spiral of self-actualizing needs for growth laid the pathway for the progressive stages in adult maturity or leadership development.

The first four needs can be satisfied in the world. They relate to conventional stages of leadership development. The fifth need to Self-Actualize is a growth need that is the turning point to post-conventional ways of being. It represents the evolutionary shift for today's world to enable us to transcend the current problems we face in our civilization. In Gandhi's words: "We must be the change we wish to see in the world."

In short, we need to develop our leadership capacity past the conventional stages of leadership development to the post-conventional stages where we begin to realize our true potential and transform the way we operate in the world to transcend current dilemmas. This turning point begins the Hero's Journey that is the timeless voyage of self-discovery and authentic power, encapsulated by Joseph Campbell in his writings on myth and legend.

Abraham Maslow	Don Beck	Richard Barrett	Ken Wilber	Suzanne Cook-Greuter	Bill Torbert & David Rooke	Antoinette Braks			
						Holist	7	Love	Soul
			Unique	Unitive	Ironist	Ironist	6	Free	Spirit
	Harmonizing Contemplative	Being of Service	Integral	Construct Aware	Magician	Alchemist	5	Care	Guidance
Self-Actualizing	Integrative Vision Logic	Making a Difference	Holistic	Autonomous	Strategist	Strategist	4	Calm	Mind
	Personalistic Relativistic	Internal Cohesion	Sensitive	Individualist	Individualist	Catalyst	3	Flow	Intuition
	Multiplistic Individualistic	Transformation	Achiever	Conscientious	Achiever	Achiever	2	Grow	Heart
Self-Esteem	Purposeful Absolutist	Self-Esteem	Mythic	Self-Conscious	Expert	Specialist	1	Play	Will
Belonging		Relationship	Warrior	Conformist	Diplomat	Conformist	0	Work	Ego
Security	Egocentric Exploitative		Magic	Self-Defensive	Opportunist	Opportunist			Instinct
Survival	Magical Animistic	Survival	Instinctual	Impulsive	Impulsive				

Progressive Stages of Development from a Range of Researchers and Consultants   [Individuate/Consolidate]

The Stages of Leadership

There are seven key stages along the spiral of leadership development that embrace current leadership capacity in the world today. They are:

1. Opportunist

2. Conformist

3. Specialist

4. Achiever

5. Catalyst

6. Strategist

7. Alchemist

The **Opportunist** is concerned with survival and security, Maslow's first two needs. The way this plays out in the world is that they are self-interested, relatively isolated and will get away with whatever they can. They operate on a day-by-day or minute-by-minute basis without a care for consequences. Their view of the world is that it is unsafe and everyone else is assumed to be an enemy. They will take what they can when they can.

The *Opportunist* lives in fear, trusts no one and largely operates in fight, flight or freeze mode. Some 5% of the Executive population is anchored at *Opportunist*. In other words, this view of the world is their Autopilot. Whenever our safety and security is threatened in the succeeding stages, it is relatively easy to regress back to the level of the *Opportunist* and resolve our situation based on self-interest alone.

The **Conformist** decides to play it safe. While they still view the world as a very challenging place to be, they believe that if they abide by all the rules and do what people in higher authority ask or tell them to do, they will be safe. They conform. They are risk averse and will only take action if instructed to do so. Most will also need a step-by-step approach mapped out for them. Their level of voluntary participation is relatively low.

In complying, *Conformists* give away their personal authentic power to positional authority. This leads to a sense of personal ineptitude that moves them to complain. In other words, when we give our personal power away to comply with others, we address this imbalance by complaining about others. If you know anyone in your workplace that complains a lot, they will be operating from a *Conformist* mindset. Some 10% of the Executive population is anchored at *Conformist* and it is the fallback position for succeeding stages in times of stress.

Conformists use reactive emotional strategies to get what they want. The three key strategies are appeasing others by being nice and bending over backwards to fit in – usually towards more senior people; controlling others by criticizing, berating and offending others - usually towards more junior people; or otherwise withdrawing from people by avoiding all communication and even eye contact.

All are unconscious emotionally manipulative techniques that produce workplace drama in the form of passive-aggressive behaviour manifesting in bullies and victims. We subconsciously base our boss-subordinate and peer-based interpersonal strategies on those we employed to get what we wanted in childhood within the comparable context of parent-child and sibling dynamics.

The **Specialist** devotes themselves to their work. They wish to develop their skills, perfect their craft and focus on the details to get everything absolutely right. They switch their primary focus from being compliant and fitting in, to standing out through the course of their work. They are experts in their field and strong contributors dotting i's and crossing t's for as long as it takes to get something right. They make up some 40% of the Executive population.

Specialists largely work individually and are focused on the quality of their work and mastery of their craft. They will drill down to the detail and ensure complete accuracy taking a comprehensive rather than pragmatic approach. A micro-manager is typically operating at the *Specialist* mindset. Their personal identity merges with their work so they take feedback very personally. They tend to be emotionally reactive when on the receiving end of constructive feedback and emotionally responsive to recognition and praise.

While the reactive behaviours are still present, they are now more associated with their work than trapped within the power struggle of the endemic parent-child and sibling dynamics. They are driven by the need to perfect their work, which is a quantum step up the spiral from *Conformist*. Focusing on increasing the quality of our own work based on our own albeit critical view of self and others, leads to continuous improvement. It is an individuation phase of leadership development. In other words it is a step out of our comfort zone into a growth zone.

As we progress through these early stages of development we take the positive attributes with us and gradually release personal reactivity based on the ego and feeling "not good enough". The stages of development form a holarchy where we gradually embrace all of who we are with awareness, understanding and kindness.

The **Achiever** is a pragmatist rather than a perfectionist. This becomes a consolidation phase for the *Specialist* when they begin to consider how their work meets the needs of colleagues, customers and clients. Their focus extends to the impact of their work rather than just the work itself.

Their goal is "fit for purpose" rather than perfect. They are open to feedback on their work, can manage change, meet deadlines, produce results and heed the customer. They make up some 30% of the Executive population.

Achievers are focused on the impact of their work and work happily with others as team players. They enjoy being in the driving seat and driving initiatives forward. They will do the right things to win, are strong performers in organizations and enjoy success. *Achievers* can also be very black and white. This enables them to be decisive and proactive albeit somewhat shortsighted compared to more advanced stages of development when life becomes shades of grey.

Customer-centric organizations try to adopt an *Achiever* mindset to create feedback loops and generate accountability for customer interactions and the customer experience. The introduction of scorecards to drive results and count wins supports the *Achiever's* competitive worldview. The world is made up of winners and losers and the *Achiever's* primary focus is to be on the winning team.

Opportunists, Conformists, Specialists and *Achievers* are all mindsets in the conventional world. They operate within conventional organizational norms. Altogether they make up 85% of the Executive population. *Specialists* and *Achievers* work extremely well <u>in</u> the world rather than <u>on</u> the world. Together they account for 70%.

The following stages in leadership development operate within post-conventional norms. This is where the hero's journey or authentic leadership begins to blossom and gradually grow into inspiring strategic leadership.

It is not a step that most organizations invite. Rather it wells up from within us when we begin to wonder what life is all about and why we do what we do. For the *Achiever* it can feel like standing on the edge of a cliff. I have found that with coaching support and a proven pathway to provide a level of certainty despite the fact that they are now moving into the world of the unknown and unchartered, they will take the step into the new realm of authentic leadership development!

The **Catalyst** is the first post-conventional stage. It is a stage of individuation, a step into a new growth zone and an unfamiliar world.

At the individuation phase of the *Specialist* we were focused on perfecting our work. At the individuation phase of the Catalyst we are focused on understanding ourselves: our motives and fears, reactions and responses, and our deepest desires and aspirations. We ask the question: "Why?"

At this stage, we move into our personal growth zone where growing and evolving becomes
our natural way of being. Even though the challenges we encounter along the way may be unfamiliar and disconcerting, for the participant, life is forever enriched. We shift from being satisfied with a life based on cause and effect to leading a purposeful and fulfilling life based on conscious intention and committed action.

Executives anchored at *Catalyst* number just 10% of the Executive population. Catalysts are focused on engaging others, igniting change and working across boundaries. Their focus turns from the impact of their work on customers and clients to the input into the design and nature of the work itself through active early engagement with all stakeholders. They are attuned to leveraging strengths, fuelling personal growth and creating best possible outcomes for the whole community.

The capacity to genuinely innovate and collaborate is initiated at *Catalyst*. At this mindset the inner world of the individual becomes more important than the external world within which they operate. In other words they heed their intuition and feelings to make decisions and generate new insights and ideas. They also listen from a much deeper place of inquiry and can therefore create a deeper connection with others and develop the ability to build trust with others.

Catalysts forge their way in the world by feeling their way forward despite uncertain circumstances. Relationships also become key as they reflect more on their own inner experience in the world and also how others feel. Many words beginning with "in" are associated with the *Catalyst* worldview: insight, innovation, intrinsic, innate, inquiry, introspection, intricate, inclusive, inquisitive, interest and intuition.

Executives anchored at **Strategists** number just 5%. This is the consolidation mode of the *Catalyst* so they will arrive here. It takes time however to become self-aware and other-aware in order to be discerning and self-validating. This time horizon can be dramatically shortened by effective coaching from the *Strategist* perspective. More on this below in relation to my research findings.

Because *Strategists* become self-validating, only they have the vision, courage and presence to generate and sustain transformational change. They have adopted the mantle of personal authentic power in the interests of serving their whole community and not just selected interest groups. This represents a shift from 'not good enough' at the *Specialist* stage, to feeling good and doing well at the *Achiever* stage, and onto focusing on the greater good for all concerned at the *Strategist* stage.

Thus, when led by a *Strategist*, the organization shifts from being customer-centric to community-centric. It succeeds in achieving medium-to-long term outcomes that make a real and significant impact on the people they serve and affect. They generate a new world through their convictions and intentions, living by their principles and in tune with their life purpose while embracing others with compassion and enthusiasm.

The mature *Strategist* is an authentic, inspiring and strategic leader. They lead confidently from the 'inside-out'. They are able to consistently stand and hold their ground while leading transformation.

The final stage that can be observed and calibrated in the post-conventional world is the *Alchemist*. They number less than 1%. They are the iconic leaders who ignite and generate social evolution as well as transform global industries. Illustrious figures such as Nelson Mandela, Oprah Winfrey, Richard Branson, Anita Roddick and Bill Gates seem to have realized their potential as *Alchemists*. The *Alchemist* seems to emerge following the far-reaching impact of their work. They are not always obvious at first but the manifestation of their aspirational intentions change the world we live in.

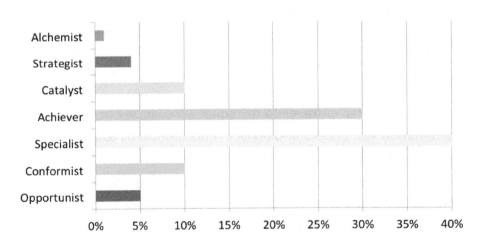

The Distribution of Executives Across the Stages

Stage Leadership Development

The theory of Stage Leadership Development suggests that while we might demonstrate behaviours at a range of levels, we are largely anchored in what we term our comfort zone or centre of gravity. This stage reflects our current beliefs and paradigms from which we operate naturally on Autopilot. When we are led and encouraged by a leader at a higher level, we can stretch more easily beyond our current level. When the opposite occurs or when we feel momentarily threatened, we can also regress, especially if we are in an individuation zone such as *Specialist* and *Catalyst*.

Stage leadership development is like a spiral. To develop our leadership capacity, we step out of our comfort zone and move into our stretch zone. Then as our new stretch zone becomes increasingly familiar, we consolidate at the next level as our new comfort zone. Thus *Specialists* will become *Achievers* as they focus on external results or the value that's created for others, and *Catalysts* will consolidate as *Strategists* as they become more self-aware and confidently bring more of their authentic voice to the world engaging with others to manifest an aspirational shared view of the future.

Through the course of traveling the spiral we change our interpretation and understanding of events around us to take increasing responsibility for whatever occurs in our world. In other words, we increasingly step into our personal power to create the world around us and learn to appreciate each and every event as an opportunity to grow, learn, heal and evolve.

Our life experience also alters. We shift from the Reactive Patterns that mark the lives of *Opportunists* and *Conformists* where life is a series of ups and downs, to the Energy Field of Creative Stretch where we take more steps forward than we do backwards. We have become goal-focused and make progress building on past efforts and achievements. This forms a large part of the life experience of the *Specialist* and more so the *Achiever*.

The *Achiever* also begins to move into the world of the Emergent Future, which is the emergence of new situations, opportunities and events that simply come up. They emerge as a result of our conscious intention and alert awareness. While the *Achiever* is taking largely familiar steps forward, the *Catalyst* is moving more proactively into the unknown and therefore exercising greater trust in what unfolds.

Once we consolidate as a *Strategist* we also engage in the Energy Field of Ease and Grace filled with surprising serendipitous events and innovative solutions where everything seems to be taken care of for us. Our pathway ahead becomes clear as our inner being is freed of all emotional reactions and unpleasantness. We are calm. Indeed my own way of describing the seven stages in developmental psychology is from **work to play, grow to flow, calm to care, and free to love**. Calm is the level of the *Strategist*.

As we transform ourselves by healing wounds and adopting more aspirational intentions, the world around us changes too. By casting our anchor to the next stage of consolidation i.e. at *Strategist* for an *Achiever*, and consciously navigating our way using the tools and techniques of a *Strategist*, we evolve.

We must also release our foundational anchor at *Conformist* by surrendering egoic drives and security needs. We learn to trust. Both avenues of growth take place simultaneously until our outside world is a reflection of our inner world. We become self-validating as we realize that every thought, belief, intention, word and action is creating our world.

Outside-In and Inside-Out

Integral Theory known as AQAL, All Quadrants and All Levels, developed by Ken Wilber, establishes four quadrants with progressive levels or stages within each. The top two quadrants relate to us as an Individual; the bottom two as a Group or collective. The left hand side focuses on the Interior or unseen, the "inside-out", how we think and feel; and the right hand side on the exterior or what is observable and tangible, the "outside-in", specific behaviors,structures, processes and systems.

I've used this theoretical framework to instigate significant and substantial change in an innovative way. Instead of taking the conventional approach and focusing on Quadrant II of Behavior to teach new skills and knowledge, I've focused on Quadrants I, Intention (Upper Left), and IV, Structure (Lower Right). I have found that by focusing on Stage Development from this combination of 'outside-in' at the organizational level and 'inside-out' on a personal level, we can accelerate our Stage Leadership Development. In other words, by imposing a higher order of structures, systems, processes and policies within which we choose to operate, and simultaneously transcending our beliefs and values to aspire to our highest version of ourselves, we can expedite our human development.

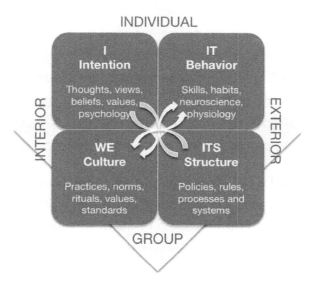

INDIVIDUAL

I **Intention** Thoughts, views, beliefs, values, psychology	**IT** **Behavior** Skills, habits, neuroscience, physiology
WE **Culture** Practices, norms, rituals, values, standards	**ITS** **Structure** Policies, rules, processes and systems

INTERIOR

EXTERIOR

GROUP

I have found that by focusing in these two areas, group structures and individual psychology, we create a shortcut to change. The underlying assumption is that we do not generally need to learn new skills or how to do things differently. Rather we need to be released from inhibiting structures and processes to adopt our natural ability to function more effectively at a higher stage of leadership capacity. Conventional organizational operating systems are holding us back and continue to constrain us notwithstanding our leadership capacity as individuals.

It's a bit like stepping into a new environment. Imagine for instance moving out of an office building full of individual offices and meeting rooms earmarked for specific activities to an open space building where you can move around freely and collaborate naturally during the course of the day. The constraints imposed by the previous rules and infrastructure, Quadrant IV, have disappeared. We didn't need to learn new skills to operate differently; we simply employ these "new" skills because we are no longer inhibited by the previous constraints.

The same is true for cultural norms imposed by more invisible structures that are the result of the frameworks and processes implicit in strategic planning, performance management, diary or calendar management, team leadership, talent management and career progression. When we transform these to align with aspirational goals and empowering processes, our strategic context changes.

When we live and work in an organization, we're bound within its structure, systems and culture. The structure provides our interconnections with other roles in terms of who's in charge of what and how we need to work with others to accomplish goals and objectives. Systems co-ordinate and automate the work to ensure a quality process and to manage risk through a system of permissions and approvals. The culture establishes the conventional ways things are done, the unwritten laws.

In most organizations these elements limit our potential to be strategic leaders, fail to leverage our strengths and aspirations to inspire others and doom us to a Groundhog Day life where everything is mundane yet absurdly stressful. Meetings generally last one hour and are scheduled back to back with the addition of intervening travel time. We operate our daily schedule to fit in as much as possible and constantly reschedule meetings as a result of requests from more senior executives or external pressures. As a result, we are extremely busy but have no real control of our time or how we are investing our conscious and limited amount of daily energy!

A second element common to many organizations is the focus on activities, deadlines and outputs. Even the highest "strategic" goals are articulated in terms of a deliverable rather than an outcome. We therefore all become caught in the world of "doing" with very limited strategic thinking on why we are doing what we're doing and little feedback on how our daily efforts are making a difference on the outcomes we'd really like to achieve and the difference we'd really like to make in the world. These structures limit us to the conventional stages of development up to and including the *Achiever*.

Sadly, we leave the power of our creativity and genius on the bench. By limiting ourselves to activities to accomplish, we never get to realize our dreams. We also lose the opportunity to embark on the hero's journey and develop self-mastery and, as a result of our lack of conscious influence, the world becomes increasingly chaotic.

A third element is the need for permission and approval. Often there is a lot of confusion around who has accountability for what, as well as significant and substantial obstacles stopping us from generating and driving new initiatives forward. It seems that every time we turn around, we need to defend ourselves or protect the people reporting to us. This puts the brake on innovation and allows risk management to become the primary focus.

As a result, we become more and more limited in what we could achieve, and our working lives become stressful and laborious. We play it safe to ensure job security while often being trapped in the parent-child dynamics implicit in boss-subordinate relationships. It is all an illusion that needs to be unveiled for us to break through as empowered adults making conscious choices that unlock our creativity and others' to build a better world.

We can circumvent this conventional operating system by working within empowering frameworks and processes instead such as the Executive Strategic Operating System I developed during the course of coaching conversations. By operating as a *Catalyst* and engaging widely with others based on guiding principles, we enable others to take real accountability and make robust decisions aligned with shared strategic direction. And gradually we can forge our own way ahead to *Strategists* through personal introspection, the development of self-awareness, emotional healing and spiritual transcendence, all of which frees us to bring our Vision, Values and Voice out to the world and make our career our Vocation.

Doctoral Research Study Findings

During 2013-14 a group of my Executive Clients agreed to participate in my PhD research study. They all undertook an assessment of their current Leadership Stage using the Mature Adult Profile (MAP) a rigorously tested Sentence Completion Assessment Instrument to calibrate Stage Development. Then they all continued in their coaching programs over a 12-month period where I introduced them to the Strategic Operating System step by step, refining it as we went.

Those who calibrated at *Achiever* and below at the beginning of the period then undertook a second MAP assessment 12 months later. I was curious as to the results as the opinions of gurus in Stage Leadership hold the view that the transformation of leadership capacity from one stage to the next ranges from 3 to 6 years, provided they are coached by a *Strategist* coach or are employed within an organization operating at this higher action logic.

It turned out that every single participant, without exception, moved a full stage, all but one to *Catalyst*, and another moved two stages direct to *Strategist* with another person knocking on its door. There was a dramatic change in the overall average leadership profile by 29 points, a full stage, in the Total Weighted Score. This came as a very welcome and total surprise to me. I had not anticipated that every single participant would move a whole Stage.

100% Stage Shift Within 12 Months Without Exception

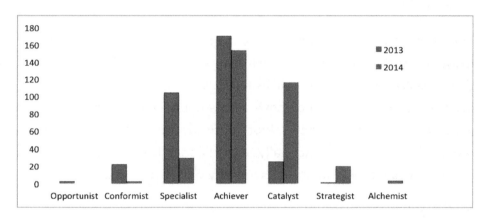

The red profile shows the range of Sentence Completions over the progressive stages in development for the group of participating clients in 2013, and the green profile represents the same group of people one year later. The range of our Sentence Completions reflects our spread around our anchoring point or centre of gravity. Sentence Completions at the post-conventional stages of *Catalyst* and *Strategist* receive a higher weighting because they originate within the individual stepping outside of organizational and social norms.

As you can see, around 50% of the Sentence Completions remained at *Achiever*. The contrast is in the marked shift from *Specialist/Conformist* Sentence Completions to *Catalyst/Strategist* Completions. The number of *Specialist* statements reduced by 23% while the number of *Catalyst* statements increased by 28%. And the number of *Conformist* statements reduced by 6%, exactly the same percentage by which the number of *Strategist* statements increased. Overall the percentage of Sentence Completions at *Opportunist*, *Conformist* and *Specialist* reduced by 30% while the percentage at *Catalyst*, *Strategist* and *Alchemist* increased by 35%!

The primary anchoring point for the majority became *Catalyst* with a fallback position at *Achiever*, while two participants shifted to *Strategist/Catalyst* in quantitative terms. One of those participants dropped a point in the qualitative assessment, which is why I use the expression: "knocking on the door" of *Strategist*. These results are remarkable given that historically Stage Leadership Development is perceived as a slow and arduous journey over a period of years.

It seems that when personal leadership development work is undertaken at an off-site leadership program, it can be quickly eroded when we return to the conventional workplace. It is very challenging to learn to embody new principles and practices of thought and action when they are not supported in our work environment.

However by implementing a new set of higher order operating frameworks and processes that demand the leadership capacity of *Catalyst* and *Strategist*, we can and do evolve. When my clients implemented an alternative set of frameworks and processes within which to operate, they all made a significant shift in Stage Development within 12 months.

It is therefore my conclusion that conventional organizational operating systems play a significant role in holding us back. To evolve, we must work from the 'inside-out" <u>and</u> adopt new operating frameworks from the 'outside-in' to support and indeed demand our evolution.

A Strategic Operating System

The quantitative findings prove that Stage Development is eminently possible within a 12-month period. The Coaching during that period was focused on creating a new Strategic Operating System ('outside-in') and also personal renewal in terms of Holistic Leadership ('inside-out'). The focus of my book, <u>Executive SOS</u>, is to illustrate and explain how the new Strategic Operating System, the supporting architecture or strategic scaffolding, served to extend and expand the leadership capacity of this group of strongly performing executives mostly at Achiever, who were keen to grow and realize their highest potential.

The 7 Steps are:

1. SCHEDULE Dynamic Diary Rhythm
2. SCOPE   Transformational Strategic Agenda
3. SCENE   Major Milestones Roadmap
4. STYLE   Values-based Leadership Culture
5. SCORE   Cascading Team Charters
6. STAGE   Compelling Signature Presentation
7. SCALE   Orchestrated Stakeholder Engagement

The Strategic Operating System (SOS) enabled my clients to discard their compliant behaviours and short-term goal focus to become

Catalysts and *Strategists* leading the way into the future. While the leadership assessments a year later provide evidence of this, so too did the extraordinary results they achieved, the transformations in their working lives and the lasting change they were able to generate in their communities. You will find their personal stories in the following chapters.

You may even venture to ask: Will it take a whole year to achieve the leadership capacity of a *Catalyst/Strategist*? My thoughts are that much of the transformation in Stage development is generated in the first few months as self-awareness is awakened and each element of the new Strategic Operating System is implemented. In other words it doesn't need to take a year – it just takes the implementation of a new architecture within which you work!

Then it requires consistent focus to author and consolidate your leadership skills and behaviors at this new level of leadership capacity. This requires significant self-awareness and new insights into interpersonal dynamics where we take greater personal responsibility for what ensures in our life experience. This is the focus of Holistic Leadership coaching from the Inside-Out. It is easier for some than others possibly due to their level of innate readiness.

We need to generate a new Autopilot to consolidate at *Strategist*. While this takes concentrated effort and attention, it becomes infinitely easier when you have the appropriate strategic scaffolding holding you in place at a higher level of potential operating capacity. The strategic scaffolding forms a tangible structure in the form of frameworks, processes, policies and principles to guide and support your actions. The Strategic Operating System is a new platform that will enable you to act significantly more strategically as a leader. It transcends conventional operating structures to leverage new research in neuroscience and the conscious power of our innate creativity to inspire others and recreate the world around us.

The Strategic Operating System (SOS) is designed to provide us with the open, emergent space for innovation and collaboration. We can customize it to suit our particular situation and leverage it to match our strengths, in order to completely alter the way we operate. In this way we can transcend the constraints of conventional structures and organizational cultures. By adopting this approach, you'll be able to introduce an empowering, engaging and transformational level of leadership that will set you apart, expand your leadership presence and ignite your career!

The more effectively you implement each dimension of the SOS, the faster you will see results in the development of your leadership capacity. It is designed to bring out your leadership potential and free you from the conventional way most organizations typically operate. And as you'll see from the success stories in the book itself, you don't need to implement each step perfectly. There will be some that will suit you more naturally than others and you can use these to leverage your growth as a leader.

All seven strategic steps are integrated and their effect is cumulative. As they each become operationalized, you will find that the interconnected templates and processes, the strategic scaffolding you put in place, builds your perspective and presence as a *Catalyst/Strategist*. It provides the open frame within which you work so that you can move into flow and consolidate at **calm**, to become an inspiring strategic leader.

Executive SOS provides the gateway to creating and sustaining a strategic agenda that is purposeful, meaningful, authentic and transformational. It opens the windows to engaging and embracing multiple stakeholders to arrive at a truly united vision and blueprint for the future. And it creates highways so that you can utilize your time every day in an orchestrated way to unlock your creativity, more than double your productivity and engage multiple stakeholders seamlessly. It will enable you to articulate your Vision, demonstrate your Values and activate your Voice so that you can live your Vocation and leave your unique personal legacy in the world that will bring about transformation.

The Strategic Operating System enables Senior Executive leaders to play their roles as *Catalysts* and *Strategists*. The growing mastery of our action orientation (AQ), emotional awareness (EQ), mindful attention (MQ) and spiritual intelligence (SQ) as we ascend the spiral can be reflected in the nature of our roles. These four ways of being: doing, relating, thinking and creating respectively associated with AQ, EQ, MQ and SQ, each transform as we develop greater leadership capacity as shown in the table.

ROLE LEVEL		S	M	L	XL	XXL
		Self	Manager	Leader	Executive	Group Exec
Developmental Stage		SPECIALIST	ACHIEVER	CATALYST	STRATEGIST	ALCHEMIST
AQ	Action Orientation	Doing	Performing	Igniting	Generating	Visionary
EQ	Emotional Awareness	Relating	Cooperating	Collaborating	Inspiring	Compassion
MQ	Mindful Attention	Thinking	Managing	Interpreting	Integrating	Wisdom
SQ	Spiritual Intelligence	Creating	Designing	Innovating	Transforming	Wizardry

When we connect shared Values with AQ, EQ, MQ and SQ, we can create a Values-based Stage-centric Leadership Model that will be psychologically robust and propel evolutionary leadership development up the spiral. It will also reflect the advantage of broad role bands allowing for significantly more fluidity, stretch and growth within each role band.

The amazing thing is that if all *Conformists*, *Specialists* and *Achievers* shifted one stage to *Specialists, Achievers* and *Catalysts*, 55% of the Executive population would have moved into post-conventional leadership. If they moved two stages to become *Achievers, Catalysts* and *Strategists*, 85% of Executive Leaders would be above the line, working <u>on</u> the world rather than <u>in</u> it. The post-conventional world would be the new norm. We would be able to transform the world to reflect our aspirations! This is precisely what we need to accomplish today. To create a better and brighter future for all humanity and life on the planet, it is urgent and essential that the majority of Executive leaders engage in Stage Development.

To find out more about Values-based Stage-centric Leadership Models, go to <u>www.antoinettebraks.com/stages</u>

Chapter 1

Run the SCHEDULE

A Dynamic Diary Rhythm

"There is more to life than simply increasing its speed."
- Mahatma Gandhi

Mastery of Time

Time is seen as one of the few limited resources we have in today's world. After all we cannot make more time than the 24 hours we have in each day. Yet most of us do not proactively manage our time so that it is aligned with our strategic goals. Instead of consciously choosing how best to invest our time, we allow meetings to invade our time. As a result we lose our strategic focus to operational issues, our boss's priorities and external concerns that appear to require our urgent and immediate attention. We're largely reactive.

Setting aside time for strategic work with all stakeholders is the primary key to discovering how to operate as an extraordinary leader on a strategic level. It is the first step to becoming a *Strategist* and joining the top 5% of Executive Leaders. When our calendar of events demands that we give attention to important strategic matters, we are pulled to make this critical first shift to becoming an inspiring, strategic leader.

By seeing your calendar or diary as a channel through which strategic work flows rather than as a limited resource that you must fit everything into, you will find that you have all the time in the world to realize your Strategic Agenda. You will stop trying to do everything that comes your way and instead empower and engage others proactively and collaboratively. Your time horizon will shift in your mind and you will soon find yourself making decisions based on your longer-term view of strategic outcomes.

Jane's Story

Jane started out as a teacher, completed a Masters in Education and was first made a Head Teacher at the young age of 27. She is a petite woman who dresses impeccably in colorful feminine-power suits, has a big heart, trusts her intuition and demonstrates conviction in her passions and purpose. You wouldn't mess with Jane! She has that matriarchal quality of highly respected school principals! Jane is a straight shooter without subterfuge.

She had just been appointed as the Executive Director in charge of Leadership and Learning for Public Schools. She was responsible for the contributions of over 1,000 people employed in her Division. Jane was committed to making the role her own and keen to take giant strides forward. She had firm views on moving out of the 1950's based schools system focused largely on academic achievement criteria and shifting to student-centric learning outcomes for the whole person based on their individual talents.

Her Division had a very high workload relative to her peers. They handled 70% of the Schools portfolio and 80% of correspondence for the Department of Education. Jane had been working weekends, as had most of her management team. There was just so much to do.

The culture in the Department could be described as risk-averse and reactive as a result of a number of factors. First, education was in the public spotlight. Parents tended to speak up whenever a policy or new criteria affected their children adversely. Secondly, small errors in the detail could have a significant detrimental impact on students and teachers. As a *result any mistakes led to casting the net for wrong doers. This put everyone on the defensive. Thirdly significant restructuring was taking place to reflect a shift in responsibility from central government decision-making to the empowerment of individual schools and regional communities. This was creating uncertainty and anxiety out in the field.*

Jane wanted a different type of organizational culture. One that was creative, forward thinking, proactive and aspirational in its goals and vision for the future. She wanted to stand strong and stand her ground to reverse the ripple effect of continuous negativity. However one of Jane's key concerns was how she addressed others who were in more senior positions. She realized she became less authentic, less audacious, and more conciliatory when talking to people who held higher positional authority.

There had also been some latitude where the more effective team members took the slack of less productive members. This inequity was beginning to seriously affect the wellbeing of the leading contributors and the morale of her management team. It was time to call a stop to it and find a way to leverage everyone's strengths while holding each person accountable for their individual contributions.

To create order out of the chaos that surrounded her and remedy the prevalent negative, defensive culture, Jane pulled her team together and activated the Dynamic Diary Rhythm within her Division. This enabled her to orchestrate time around a Strategic Agenda and a desired culture in collaboration with her management team members and other stakeholders. The proactive management of time was the key turning point from being overloaded and frantic albeit effective, to becoming visionary and empowering as a more strategic and inspiring leader.

By proactively putting time aside for strategic thinking and the development of a more positive corporate culture, Jane actively influenced the development of a new Strategic Agenda. With her leadership, the people in her Division began to change the prevailing culture by embodying a more positive perspective. Jane invited everyone to start looking forward to progress and possibilities rather than in the rear view mirror awaiting complaints and recriminations.

She then also set about holding her ground in terms of her management team members meeting their individual performance expectations. Jane did this by using the Courageous Caring Conversation model to give voice to patterns of behaviour along with their effect on the interpersonal dynamics and corporate culture. She also carefully articulated specific behavioral and performance expectations for the people involved while supporting and encouraging their growth and development.

Jane was careful to hold the same conversation with relevant stakeholders inside and outside her Division so that her intentions were clearly articulated and understood by everyone. This was a major breakthrough in terms of overcoming her previous acquiescence in the presence of more senior people.

While her principal battles were to hold course on their agreed Strategic Agenda and demand performance from all members of her team equitably, Jane did not stop there. She also focused on their development. She ensured there were stretch opportunities available for those people who were eager to learn and grow. Even when she was criticized for developing others as a discretionary investment of time and resources that was not absolutely essential given the high workload, she stuck to her convictions.

Halfway through the coaching period Jane re-instigated her

*focus on her own wellbeing in relation to the mastery of time.
No meetings after 4pm, and out of the office by 6pm every day.
Orchestrating time was of the essence to increase strategic
focus, leverage her innate productivity and assure her personal
wellbeing. She fine-tuned the Dynamic Diary Rhythm to ensure
that the strategic intent and values culture cascaded beyond
the Executive Team to reach all members of her Division. The
conscious orchestration of time and strategic focus held them
together on a common path.*

*Jane succeeded in shifting her Division's culture and
performance despite challenging political alliances and issues
that could have derailed her in her aspiration to create a high
performing organization. Her commitment to her Strategic
Agenda and Dynamic Diary Rhythm, and dedication and
determination to be authentic and stand strong, enabled her
Division to become a positively charged high performing unit.*

*Jane blossomed as the confident, inspiring and visionary leader
she was within. Her courageous authenticity and spiritual
integrity shone through. As a result she ignited
transformational change all around her, regardless of seniority.
She took the lead on the Strategic Agenda for Education
because she chose to influence and lead others rather than
because it was in her role description mainly composed of
activities to accomplish. Her beautiful 'Thank you' card at the
end of our Coaching Program summed things up for her.*

> *"Dear Antoinette, This is just a small way of saying thank
> you for your guidance, direction and clarity of ideas and
> general "enlightenment" about myself over the last year.
> Your wise counsel has been appreciated more than you
> know. Thank you. Best wishes, Jane."*

*Jane's potential had been locked within her. By deciding to be
the leader she knew she could be, and taking the first masterful*

step to devote herself to exercising strategic leadership, she unlocked her creativity, cast aside her doubts and rose to a position of authentic power well beyond the remit of her role.

A DYNAMIC DIARY RHYTHM

*"Whenever you find yourself on the side of the majority,
It is time to pause and reflect."*
- Mark Twain

In the busy, busy world of a typical Senior Executive, meetings largely run your workday. Work is done before each meeting by members of your team in terms of emails, proposals, reports and presentations, and afterwards to follow up with action items that will inform relevant stakeholders of progress and next steps.

People arrive, they talk to each other and leave. That's a meeting. People may ask questions, inquire into situations, influence others, propose new ideas, explore alternatives, appreciate minority views, express dissatisfaction or concerns, or otherwise be silent allowing the weight of opinion to land on a decision or not. Many meetings are surplus to requirements, boring and uneventful or entertaining yet unproductive. They are the bane of many an executive's life!

Each day and week becomes more and more chaotic as meetings shift to meet the changing needs of more senior people, deadlines shift to accommodate delays and resources, and new urgent matters come up that demand immediate attention. Everything is constantly shifting. Executive Assistants can easily spend up to 80% of their time rescheduling meetings as a result of these continuous changes. Many have turned this into an art form and see their key performance outcome as ensuring that their executive has met the needs of as many senior people and stakeholders as possible! Their mantra seems to be, the busier they are, the better!

Constantly Shifting Priorities Is Unproductive

The Senior Executive meanwhile is chasing their tail from one meeting to the next scheduled back-to-back like buzzing bees that hover from one flower to the next, always moving. Their intentions are good. They endeavor to realize shared goals and outcomes, or simply focus on getting the work done in record time at the required standard. However it is impossible to operate as a *Strategist* in this urgent prism of constant change.

Because their Management Team Meetings and 121 meetings with their team members are totally within their own control, they are invariably postponed or canceled to accommodate more senior people. Therefore the people in their own Division also become more reactive in their approach to their work. Managing by dispatching urgent emails, quick fire phone calls and chasing others to catch them on the fly becomes the norm.

It is essential to break free of this madness! How amazing would it be to run a concerted series of meetings with a focused agenda that built positive momentum? Where you were operating on autopilot knowing exactly how you would be spending your time each day every week! Where order instead of chaos reigned!

Break Free of The Madness!

The Dynamic Diary Rhythm is designed to orchestrate your

meetings over the course of time with 80% of all types of meetings scheduled at least a year in advance. It becomes the key integrator of all your work. Instead of allowing your work to direct what you do, you choose to give priority to how frequently you engage with various types of stakeholders and on what subject areas with whom. Your schedule becomes a channel like a series of highways through which content flows.

This changes everything! It gives priority to empowering your people and collaborating with your stakeholders while focusing on the iterative development of a strong and robust Strategic Agenda. Instead of your schedule or diary being a limited resource to fit in as much as possible, your schedule becomes a channel through which selected content flows, engaging with the relevant people over the course of time. Your time is orchestrated to generate breakthrough results!

Concerted engagement with others is a key defining element of a leader operating at the stages of *Catalyst* and *Strategist*. At the previous *Specialist* and *Achiever* levels, it is the work that drives us on a daily basis. Seeing your role as being accountable for engagement rather than achievement is a key strategic shift in how you approach your role. Instead of the work coming first and adjusting your time commitments to manage the workload, engagement comes first and you set your time commitments to the people you must engage and embrace to realize your Strategic Agenda.

Concerted Engagement Comes First; Work Second

Neuroscience helps us to become enormously productive. It really is very simple. We all know that when we drive to a familiar place such as home, we often seem to get there without thinking. We have no memory of what occurred, we have simply arrived home safe and sound. We have driven home on our Autopilot. Our brain has learned the route home and can get us there without conscious endeavor.

As soon as something unusual or unexpected comes up, such as an officer diverting traffic, it alerts our rational brain, the neocortex, and we can focus on taking necessary conscious action. If something threatening comes up, our reptilian brain, the amygdala, leaps into action and we can take emergency action without conscious thought except to stay alive! Our brain works automatically in relation to what we perceive and how we interpret the situation before us.

Our Autopilot is a Very Valuable Mental Capacity

Now imagine travelling on an unfamiliar route. This requires our conscious mental attention. We need to be on the alert as everything around us is new and different. We need to think about which lane to travel in, if there are bicycle lanes and pedestrian crossings to watch out for, which roads and exits to take, if and when we can make a right hand turn etc

When we use our conscious energy in this way, it seems to take much longer to get to our destination the first time, and we get tired more quickly. However once we've repeated the journey a number of times and it becomes more familiar, our Autopilot starts to take over, and we appear to arrive at our destination in no time at all!

Your Calendar is a Highway

Now imagine that your calendar is the pathway to your destination. If it is different every day of the week and from week to week, it requires a lot of conscious attention to navigate each day. Each day appears to be longer and more tiring because it is different. The opposite also holds true. If there is a repeating rhythm to your diary each week, you can navigate it without even thinking about it.

This is important for two reasons. First, we only have so much conscious energy, will power or mental focus to expend each day. Our will power diminishes as it becomes used up throughout the day and our mental focus deteriorates if we have been jumping around from subject to subject. Stress levels go up and we become tired. Do this consistently and we become exhausted, burnt out.

Thus the first key element of the Dynamic Diary Rhythm is consistency! Day-by-day, week-by-week, month-by-month and quarter-by-quarter, we can set up a pattern of meetings that we learn to navigate on Autopilot. This frees our mental energy to focus on content and context rather than the route we take each day. As a result we can become much more strategic, make better important decisions and more than double our own productivity!!

Consistency is Key to the Dynamic Diary Rhythm

I first discovered the power of consistency in my early career working as a Search and Selection Consultant with Australasian recruitment firm and market leader Morgan and Banks. I worked from 7am to 6pm every day like clockwork. While colleagues worked longer hours, it turned out that I became the highest performing consultant in the business even though I was a newbie.

I simply scheduled the Morgan and Banks success formula into my diary religiously and set up my meetings well in advance every Monday morning. I met with three clients each week on

Tuesday, Wednesday and Thursday mornings, and with 20 candidates each week during the afternoons at 2, 3, 4 and 5pm. I completed their Profile Reports first thing the following morning between 7 and 9am.

I followed exactly the same course of action every week running about ten retained assignments each quarter. It was a rhythm that I tuned into. It meant I could use all my conscious energy identifying, assessing, shortlisting and negotiating with candidates to meet my clients' needs. I did not vary my schedule one iota. I was rested and well, in flow. Much to my own surprise, I became the highest performer in the company within 18 months of joining the Sydney office.

We Can Become Highly Productive High Performers

More recently I was a member of the Assessment Team with Hudson Talent Group in an intensive Management Development Centre for the most Senior Executives in the Public Sector in New South Wales. Each day consisted of a highly concentrated, intense series of assessment, reporting and calibration activities.

I consciously set up an Autopilot so that I could navigate each day effortlessly. Once set up and mastered, my productivity increased enormously. I was personally amazed at the fluidity of the day and fluency of my mind. I could sit down and articulate a valid and insightful assessment in just a few minutes, as I had nothing else to think about. My mind and body worked on Autopilot. While I would finish by 8pm each day without feeling stressed, other consultants stayed till 10pm or took work home.

After I went away for a week halfway through the Development Centre, I was curious to see how I would go on my return. The result was astonishing. Not only did my Autopilot switch on immediately, but I also became even more insightful and astute in my assessments!! My thoughts traveled from mind to tapping fingers instantaneously. I even found myself completing early and enjoying a cup of tea during the course of the day!! This was completely out of the question for any of my fellow assessors!

The first secret is to set up a consistent Diary Rhythm in order to navigate on Autopilot and free your mind to do the actual work itself effortlessly.

Our Autopilot Frees Our Mind to Work Effortlessly

Secondly, our brain works at different frequencies. Busy Beta is our normal alert consciousness when we are awake and focused on specific tasks and activities. We tune into active Alpha when we are relaxed, calm, lucid and in flow. Our thoughts are emergent and our intuition is activated. At the next frequency level are reflective Theta waves where we are deeply relaxed as in meditation. And we slip into dreamy Delta when we are asleep.

When we rush around, we're in busy Beta. When we sit in 60-minute meetings going through an insurmountable list of items to address, we're in busy Beta. When we're scanning our emails or reviewing the work of others to get as quickly as possible to the end, we tend to be in busy Beta. However, when we take more time out for an open space meeting to discover and explore a particular subject matter, we can move into active Alpha. We realize an optimal state to innovate and collaborate when we are in an active Alpha frequency rather than in busy Beta.

We Tend to Rush Around in Busy Beta

When our brain waves are at the Alpha frequency we are open to others, open to ideas and open to new possibilities. Different parts of our brain get activated. We can do this more easily if we meditate daily. However the structure of time also assists significantly. When we go into a 90-minute meeting with an open albeit structured agenda, our brain more easily opts to move into active Alpha.

We are then free to innovate and collaborate, see alternative views and identify new possibilities and transcendent solutions. In Alpha, our minds and hearts open. We can envisage a better future, see into perplexing dilemmas and better understand the feelings and experiences of others. We become significantly more insightful and creative.

Innovation and Collaboration are Activated in Alpha

Our brain enjoys the optimal experience of being at the Alpha frequency for approximately 90 minutes, and then it prefers to take a 15-minute rest to process and classify the new neural pathways that have been ignited. This is why offsite workshops often run in a series of 90-minute sessions interspersed with intervening activities.

Therefore, as a Senior Executive who wants to become an inspiring strategic leader, your ideal Dynamic Diary Rhythm is composed of 90-minute meetings to facilitate open, strategic, insightful conversation with 30-minute intermissions to review emails, make phone calls, travel to meetings or carry out administrative tasks. As long as the brain is doing something different and less demanding, it is happy to dual process.

Schedule 90-minute Meetings with 30-minute Intervals

So the second key dimension of the Dynamic Diary Rhythm to unlock your creativity and double your productivity is to set up your diary in 90-minute meetings with 30-minute intervals. This has the power to activate the Alpha brain frequency capability and provides sufficient time to focus on content and context, principles and purpose. Meetings become much more meaningful and interconnected. They build momentum.

By setting up your schedule well in advance in an orderly fashion with specific times devoted to different types of meetings for your organization, for executive and management teams, and with direct reports, colleagues and stakeholders, you will soon establish your own Autopilot. And the intervening 30-minute time slots will become enormously valuable to cover off emails, administrative tasks, phone calls, travel and any unexpected events that arise during the day.

Thirdly, by moving away from the list approach for your Meeting Agendas and shifting to an open structured Agenda, you will be able to facilitate strategic, exploratory conversations. As a Senior Executive it is essential to invite thoughts, comments, ideas and suggestions in a proactive, empowering way in order to discern and develop a shared understanding of the strategic context. This ensures that the important strategic work of the organization receives attention and that everyone's strategic focus is aligned.

Open Structured Meeting Agendas Are Also Key

The net effect is that as time goes on you will find that deadlines and major events gradually integrate with your prescribed pattern of engagement. They become fused.

Everything will be much more interconnected and you will find that you can delete, delegate or delay work much more easily in alignment with your strategic priorities. Simultaneously, as you set and hold your own boundaries and priorities, the work that flows around you changes to reflect your intentions. You will feel more liberated each and every day rather than stressed by what is happening around you.

Rather than be a limited resource, time becomes elastic. Accompanied by the power of conscious intention activated in Alpha, your mind will expand its capacity to match your timeframe and time will stretch to match your work production. Thus you become more creative, more productive, more strategic and more inspiring. You will experience an enlivening sense of purpose and passion and know with confidence that the work you do each day is clearly creating your vision for tomorrow.

Time Stretches, Your Mind Expands and Work Adjusts

"Time is an illusion."
- Albert Einstein

KEY IDEAS

1. A consistent Dynamic Diary Rhythm activates our Autopilot to navigate our schedule so that we can use our daily quotient of conscious energy on the strategic content and context of our work.

2. 90-minute Meetings with 30-minute intervals provides us with the opportunity to activate the Alpha frequency essential for strategic work while optimizing our opportunity to manage transactional work during the interim periods.

3. Consistent open structured agendas for the 90-minute Meetings activate open and insightful dialogue leading to genuine engagement, thoughtful inquiry, empowerment of participants, innovation and collaboration.

4. An orchestrated Dynamic Diary Rhythm leads to stress-free living, significant increases in creativity and productivity, and the ability to achieve medium term high performance strategic outcomes with the least effort.

For more information on Stage Leadership Development, go to www.antoinettebraks/stages

For more information on Executive SOS, go to www.antoinettebraks/SOS

Chapter 2

Define the SCOPE

A Transformational
Strategic Agenda

"The greater danger is not that our hopes are too high, and we fail to reach them. It's that they are too low, and we do." - **Michelangelo**

Mastery of Vision

The problem with focusing on increasing profits and building market share (private sector) or decreasing costs and reducing dependency (public sector) as primary indicators of performance, is that we don't aspire to anything great. We simply maximize opportunity or diminish challenge in the current world with a primary focus on financial indicators rather than give thought to creating a much better world.

A mark of the *Strategist*, the type of leader who has a broad and far reaching Strategic Agenda, is that they choose to and are able to transform the world around them. They aspire to great results that benefit the greater good of all people. Their commitment to their aspirations to make a significant difference in uplifting the wellbeing and capacity of their customers, clients and communities of people they reach and touch, ignites the personal aspirations of the people they lead.

Further, it turns out that aspirational organizations who put people first, both within and the people they serve, offer us amazing success stories. They have grown significantly faster than their competitors, sustained strong levels of growth and profitability over a long period of time and have been recognised as sought after workplaces, developers of community spirit and instigators of far-reaching social transformation.

To be an inspiring, strategic leader, we must set our sights high. Our Strategic Agenda must be transformational! It must be purposeful rather than just functional, visionary rather than an extrapolation of today based on yesterday, and it must incorporate progressive strategic shifts in performance and culture that are clearly articulated.

This enables people to set off on a journey of possibility notwithstanding the VUCA world of volatility, uncertainty, complexity and ambiguity that we live in today. A Transformational Strategic Agenda transcends the present and promises a brighter and better future.

Richard's Story

Richard was the CIO of Fire & Rescue NSW supporting over 100,000 rescue workers. He was frequently not finishing work until 9pm and he was tired and at times felt exhausted. He spent just about all of his time in the detail of elaborate planning, flawless implementation and rigorously reviewing what had taken place – whether it was a major software upgrade or his personal holiday to see the North Pole!

He was steeped in the minutiae because he was afraid of anything going wrong and wanted to make the most of every opportunity. When you're responsible for the systems that reassure everyone in the community that they're safe in a country where bush fires and floods are increasing annually and people's lives are genuinely in jeopardy, you have to be certain that everything is working as perfectly as possible! The mantra for his IT Division was "Better Systems, Safer Communities."

He was also a relatively demure and reticent person who was not as resilient as he knew he could be. Richard was self-critical and simultaneously, as is always the case, also acknowledged that he was often critical of others. As a softly spoken, reserved and considered person, he was reticent to voice his true opinions and relatively easy to overlook.

Notwithstanding his demure demeanor, or perhaps as a counterfoil to his protective approach, Richard was also quite savvy. He had developed many strategies to encourage collaboration without needing to overtly persuade or influence others directly. For instance, against the odds, he successfully encouraged five agencies to onboard his systems by carefully determining and articulating acceptable win-win outcomes for *all the parties. He frequently employed this method to instigate new initiatives, progress projects and improve the capability of his client agencies.*

In summary, Richard was a very astute man who operated almost exclusively behind the scenes. This had worked for him up to this point, but now he had a larger vision and needed to present his ideas to Senior Executives to persuade them to support his aspirational vision of the future. This was a significant challenge for him and he didn't quite know how to approach it.

First, I invited Richard to discard his personal critic and instead appreciate our humanity by thinking along the lines of: "Everyone's doing the best they can." This was an important breakthrough to enable him to talk more confidently and kindly to others, and better appreciate his own vulnerability in a positive way. He also just needed to do the best he could with awareness of self and others in each present moment.

Secondly, we realized that his underlying sense of job insecurity as a result of possible failure in the future was causing him undue anxiety. We averted this by reviewing the reality of his career. He had not "failed" previously and there was no rational reason to suppose he might in the future. In fact, he had a history of continuing success, growing acknowledgement and career advancement.

Then we added affirmations to this that were true and authentic but had not been part of his inner conversation. "My career is safe and secure. My team is extraordinary. My work speaks for itself. I am amazingly effective at what I do." Expressed in a heartfelt way to himself, these words were not arrogant. Quite the opposite. They were self-affirming in a humble and aspirational way. They reminded Richard of his effectiveness as an Executive. As a result, he began to take on board the reality of his considerable contribution to his organization.

These personal interventions were essential for Richard to tap into his professional aspirations. Criticism of self and others, fear of the future and commonly held feelings of insecurity and inadequacy sabotage us. Affirmations assist in retraining our mind to a different perspective so that we demonstrate more self-confidence, while other cognitive and heart-based processes enable us to release negative thought patterns.

Next, and most significantly for Richard, we began to create a structured Transformational Strategic Agenda around his Vision of the future, the higher purpose for his organization, key strategic outcomes and the implicit transformational shifts that would be necessary to bring about the new world. They could also cause significant upheaval. You see, Richard had big ideas. Not just ideas that would improve things as they were. No. Audacious visionary ideas that would entirely transform the way IT systems supported Fire & Rescue. Ideas that would have a major impact on the current workforce and their technology suppliers. If he was not able to truly inspire others, he was bound to meet with considerable resistance.

We went through the Agenda setting process one step at a time, from Purpose to Strategic Shifts in Performance and Culture, a Scorecard of KPIs and a series of Strategic Initiatives that would enable everyone to see the bigger picture, the pathway ahead and indeed the transformational vision that Richard had in mind. By using the Transformational Strategic Agenda Framework, he was able to articulate the journey that lay ahead so that others could also envisage the future destination he had in mind and how they could get there.

Today Richard has revolutionized the workforce, their approach to technology and is working with global technology partners to create a 21st century Emergency Management System that anticipates issues through analytics and artificial intelligence, thereby averting danger for people and property. 'MIINDER' is a network-wide solution designed for real time reporting to anticipate danger, enable cross-agency collaboration, distribute rescue workers more strategically and facilitate more informed, predictive decision-making to protect people and property from the imminent risks of bush fires and floods. Instead of just responding effectively to immediate and pending danger, the organization will be poised to avert danger. This was a breakthrough transformational approach!

As a result of his inspiring, strategic leadership, Richard has been invited to make many presentations to large audiences of professionals within his industry and beyond. Notwithstanding his quiet, humble manner, he is consistently scoring significantly higher ratings at these conferences than other speakers due to his breadth of vision and passion for the new world he is creating. The light in his eyes shines brightly and his voice resonates with commitment and confidence. In his presentations, Richard excites and enchants others to see what a much better, brighter and safer world it will be when his futuristic vision is realized.

His Strategic Agenda is transformational; his vision extraordinary. Richard has stood his ground and in fact ploughed new fields of opportunity with courage and conviction.

He has recently received a number of awards for innovation, project delivery and leading-edge initiatives. Recognition has come from his Agency, the emergency services industry and Government. His inspirational and transformational agenda has even reached the Wall Street Journal in an article celebrating the innovative predictive system conceived by Richard's Vision of what was possible.

In his own words:

> "At first I was stressed, in a rut, putting in a mega effort, fatigued, not that happy ... you identified the drivers, fear of not doing a good enough job, trying to do both the strategic work and the doing work. You encouraged me to do more of what I enjoy and less of the rest which led to a restructure, empowering my direct reports, and adopting the new reality that I am actually really good at what I do. I developed more confidence in my success.
>
> There used to never be a moment when I wasn't doing something. Now it's ok to pause, look around, be satisfied with the moment and start to see a better future.
>
> You helped me deal with difficult relationships, helped me with personal confidence, and developing a leadership presence, and lastly, reminded me of what I already knew but had lost, my personal wish to get closer to God and to take actions to get out of the mire I was in.
>
> I no longer feel the need to read all my emails ... now I'm surfing the chaos ... starting to become a very different person from what I used to be. ... I'm more confident, relaxed, calm and self-assured ... giving up control, giving up striving, surrender is key to the process ...
>
> I rejoice in other people getting the credit, it really doesn't matter who gets the credit as long as we achieve amazing things ... and you provided great business collateral especially strategic business engagement, use of strategic scaffolding, empowering people to make the right decisions, and the energy fields around us in terms

of interpersonal dynamics.

I learnt how to get through things with self-respect intact, and greater assurance, so next time something might arise, I know I can handle it."

Richard's manager is a high performer who demands high performance from her executive team and does not give praise lightly. A positive if not glowing performance review therefore carries great weight. She writes:

"An excellent year of achievements - delivery and planning – that places us well for the future. Projects remain well run and within time and budget.

Richard, you bring extraordinary vision to your work and are highly successful at bringing Executives and staff along with you. The range and scope of the IT program is a result of this vision and collaboration.

Thank you for your ongoing contribution to the organization. I am pleased you have found the coaching so rewarding."

Richard went from being a reticent and somewhat stressed person in a bit of a rut to becoming a recognized innovative and transformational industry leader. Through the course of framing his Strategic Agenda and articulating the Transformational Shifts that were implicit in his view of the future, Richard developed a confident and powerful personal presence that inspired others.

He did not change his personality. Rather he opened up to his Vision. Richard reconfigured his Division so that he would be free to focus on an aspirational Strategic Agenda that he was passionate about. He opened his heart to himself and people in general so that he was more open to meeting an audience with personal authenticity as an enthusiastic advocate using his

Compelling Signature Presentation. And he opened his mind to his intrinsically creative superpowers to bring forth a new world of smart 21st century technology. 'Better Systems To Create Safer Communities.'

Richard is happily fulfilling his purpose to create a better world. His emergence as a leading voice and creator of the future was both an exhilarating and emotional journey that elevated his leadership presence, expanded his reach and enabled him to realize his aspiration to make a significant contribution to the community he serves.

A TRANSFORMATIONAL

STRATEGIC AGENDA

Whatever you can do or dream you can, begin it.
Boldness has genius, power and magic in it. Begin it now.
- Von Goethe

Most organizations invest time in strategic planning. However many begin with the typical SWOT analysis of Strengths, Weaknesses, Opportunities and Threats that limits thinking to the current situation and extrapolates from there. It is strategic in terms of making choices that trade off present needs with future goals amongst competitive players, and there is strategy implicit in deciding how best to go about achieving those goals, but this does not constitute a Transformational Strategic Agenda.

It is a Competitive Strategic Agenda at best. It looks sideways and at impending strife to craft a winning strategy, reflecting the *Achiever's* approach to compete, strive and win, rather than focusing on creating a better future as would a *Strategist*. A strategic plan based on achieving more profitable goals more effectively and efficiently does not create a better world. It is built on the *Achiever* mentality of doing more and competing with others to achieve more rather than create anew.

Further, a "Plan" consists largely of doing. It doesn't tend to start with futuristic outcomes that create a better world. And often when futuristic outcomes are set through the course of 'blue sky' or 'blue ocean' thinking, they quickly convert into activities or initiatives, things to do to execute the strategy. Strategic thinking goes directly from a future view into an action plan from the Executive Suite down.

Activity-based Strategic Plans Lock Up Our Potential

When we wish to transform the world, a plan just doesn't cut it! Transformation entails a journey, a hero's journey, where we move into the unknown and can generally only see the next step in front of us even while we envisage the future. If we know all the steps in advance, then by definition, this is simply a plan of action. It's not a transformational journey and will not produce transformational outcomes. Moving into the unknown requires Vision, Values and Voice.

When we wish to transform the world, we must aspire to the greatest vision we can imagine. As Einstein said: "Logic will get you from A to B. Imagination will take you everywhere." Once we can imagine something and we commit to its realization, we attract the resources, opportunities and partners to make it a reality. To do this while leading an organization or large division within an enterprise, we need to communicate clearly and consistently articulating the purpose, high level performance KPIs and strategic shifts we know are necessary to realize our Vision.

A most engaging and enlightening strategic thinking process can be wrapped around the Appreciative Inquiry methodology called SOAR. S for Strengths and O for Opportunities retain part of the SWOT framework, while Weaknesses and Threats are superceded by Aspirations and Results. Community-wide engagement using SOAR has yielded phenomenal results across many diverse sectors.

Not only do we need to articulate the Vision of the future, we also need to give Voice to the journey. Executive leaders with a Vision and a Plan can be effective *Achievers*. They make up some 30% of the Executive population. Executive leaders with a Vision and a Voice who are prepared to be authentic and vulnerable can be remarkable *Catalysts* (just 10% of executive leaders) and ultimately lead as *Strategists* (top 5%), the stage of leadership capacity that equips us to generate transformational outcomes.

Move Into the Unknown with Vision, Values and Voice

Time and again I see Purpose, Mission or Vision Statements that are boring, functional and uninspiring. They do not lead to a new tomorrow, they simply describe today's role. Some are egoic, others platonic, and some even sardonic. These statements are put up on wall posters, documented in the Annual Report or appended to email signatures as tag-lines. Despite their visibility, they are silent. They become a byline! Uninspiring words cannot come alive through expression or active usage.

Whereas inspiring Purpose Statements become iconic!! Nike: "Just Do It." L'Oreal: Because You're Worth It." BP: "Beyond Petroleum." They need to be imbued with a sense of restless passion and inspiring vision that will open up the opportunity to take a quantum leap in creating a better world. The development of a bold Purpose Statement unleashes our power to operate at a higher order of co-creative endeavor.

Indeed by activating the Purpose Statement using the most

vital and vibrant words within it to mark the strategic focus of each year, it lifts our eyes to the horizon and becomes increasingly alive over a 3-5 year period. It has the power to hold the strategic themes for the years ahead and genuinely contribute to a masterful campaign to transcend limits and move mountains!

Purpose Statements Need To Be Iconic!

The scope of the Transformational Strategic Agenda is first defined by an aspirational, uplifting Purpose Statement. Without such a statement, the frame within which we operate is constrained and we are limited to transactional efforts to get the job done. That frame either creates a prison around our mind and spirit or transcends the present to lift us up and surrender into our own potential greatness. It either limits or stimulates our growth and our intrinsic power to make a much more significant difference in the world.

In addition to an uplifting and inspiring Purpose Statement, we also need to identify the Transformational Strategic Shifts that will enable a much greater performance in the future. Without strategic shifts we become stuck in business-as-usual. We can focus on continuous improvement making things slightly more efficient or effective at various points of the process, but this will not lead to generating transformational outcomes. We must articulate and appreciate what these strategic paradigm shifts require of us as leaders.

Strategic Shifts Lead To Transformational Outcomes!

Richard's Purpose Statement, while more succinct than most, "Better Systems, Safer Communities", is open-ended and community orientated. His set of principles to guide decision making were encompassed in the Key Strategic Performance and Culture Shifts he determined were essential to create the next generation of Fire & Rescue systems and services.

Those principles were: de-duplicate, simplify and automate. These three principles alone in the context of the broader strategic frame of outcome-based KPIs were sufficient to guide decision-making so that his team of executives was empowered to take accountability for leading their teams decisively and confidently into the future.

Shared Principles and Paradigms Guide Decision-Making

This is in stark contrast to a set of business plans documenting a series of actions and activities. If we define everything we do by what we do rather than by why we do it and how we need to operate differently, we are not operating as empowered Senior Executives. We're just human resources doing our work day-in day-out like wind-up toys moving along a linear path. This is neither stimulating, rewarding nor meaningful.

I ask my clients to identify three strategic shifts in Performance that will enable the business to achieve significantly better results for customers or outcomes in the broader community. They could include the need to integrate service delivery, centralize services around the customer or community, develop new funding sources, integrate with other market sectors and/ or procure and implement new technologies.

Secondly I invite them to identify three strategic shifts in Culture, in the way people engage and work together, that will support the opportunity to realize the desired visionary performance. Shifts in Culture relate to the people, both within the organization and in relation to stakeholder engagement. By clarifying the three key quantum shifts required, the organization is able to move along a transformational pathway.

Often these strategic culture shifts include the need for leadership development, increased professional excellence, wider engagement with stakeholders as partners and the development of a values-based culture. This work leads to the clarification of the key principles and values that must be adopted to ignite these strategic shifts. Strategic culture shifts generally precede strategic performance shifts.

Transformational Strategic Shifts Open Up the Gateway

These strategic shifts become clear when articulated as annual stepping-stones across key themes and a set of guiding principles. Each year represents a progressive step to the following year. The cumulative effect of these strategically chosen new foundations that will create the platform for the future is like an emergent wave from the ocean that builds in momentum and then hurls itself back into the ocean changing forever everything in its wake.

Without multiple streams of transformational strategic initiatives that interconnect with each other, there is insufficient momentum and we end up with business-as-usual. The tide of a lake rises and falls in a similar way. Little changes. We need to create momentum by articulating a campaign, learn how to crest as a wave does on the rise and bring all stakeholders along with us as we surf the wave that leads to our desired future.

Creating strategic focus in this way ensures that the entire executive team shares in the shaping of the Strategic Agenda. It is not something that can be configured alone. It is not the amalgamation of individual agendas stitched together. It requires thought, dialogue, inquiry, insight and collaboration on what is strategically most essential in the most powerful sequence leading to a primary emphasis that is the hallmark of significant and substantial performance in each progressive year.

Shape Your Strategic Agenda Through Collaboration

All of these strategic shifts in the way the work is done, for whom it is done or how it is done, require strategic leadership by all members of the Executive Team. They demand strategic thinking and strategic focus, much more than the typical strategic planning processes that we've become accustomed to. Instead of empowering us to realize audacious goals, conventional methods enslave us to what must be fixed or finished.

Life is meant to be much more fun than completing a list of job activities. This is okay for people who are new to the work in hand. They need to learn the ropes. But as we take on more responsibility as Senior Executives, we can be much more than traffic directors. We can become strategic architects so that we can lead the generation of transformational outcomes for our customers and communities, the people we serve today and future generations.

If we want to travel the world, we need to fly across countries. If we want to uplift our world, we need to fly across boundaries. There is no point being in the trenches! That will not get us very far! We need to get up in the air and learn how to fly! By lifting our strategic perspective and defining the scope of our work based on a Transformational Strategic Agenda encompassing purposeful strategic shifts in performance and culture, we uplift everyone around us and create the opportunity for our mutual collaborative and innovative potential to blossom.

Lifting Our Strategic Frame Uplifts Everyone!

When you are inspired by some great purpose, some extraordinary project, all your thoughts break their bonds: Your mind transcends limitations, your consciousness expands in every direction, and you find yourself in a new, great and wonderful world. Dormant forces, faculties and talents become alive, and you discover yourself to be a greater person by far than you ever dreamed yourself to be. - **Patanjali**

KEY IDEAS

1. A strategic plan of action does not empower executives or advance civilization. It limits our potential to grow and our capacity to create a better world.

2. Creating a better world requires a bold purpose and vision of the future and an appreciation of the requisite strategic shifts in performance and culture.

3. Purpose Statements must articulate an audacious and aspirational intention that makes work meaningful and worthwhile to ignite our human potential to make a significant difference in the world.

4. Strategic Culture and Performance Shifts help us to navigate our journey ahead by consciously transforming our leadership capacity to realize transformational outcomes.

For more information on Stage Leadership Development, go to www.antoinettebraks/stages

For more information on Executive SOS, go to www.antoinettebraks/SOS

Chapter 3

Set the SCENE

A Major Milestones Roadmap

"The real voyage of discovery lies not in seeking new landscapes but in having new eyes." - Marcel Proust

Mastery of Focus

Earlier I wrote about the flood of emails, constant meetings and urgent deadlines that executives deal with daily. This sense of overwhelm is induced by trying to keep a grasp of all the minutiae that you previously dealt with as a middle manager. You see your role as ensuring that good decisions are made rather than focusing on the results to be achieved and milestones to be met. You haven't yet extricated yourself from the day-to-day decision-making and therefore find yourself 'managing' on the run by intervening on a host of matters through the course of the day.

The problem is that this leads to you being a bottleneck. The people around you feel that they need to consult with you before taking decisions because if they don't, they run the risk of being corrected later requiring rework and loss of face. Notwithstanding the fact that you are a good decision-maker, now, as a Senior Executive, it's time to focus on the bigger picture. Most Senior Executives remain largely concerned with operational matters such as ensuring that project deliverables are met and interpersonal dilemmas are resolved because that is their comfort zone.

The problem is, instead of being responsible for the work of one team or division, you now have anywhere between five and ten numbering upwards of 1000 people! If we continue to manage and lead others as a Senior Executive in the same way we did as a middle manager, team or project leader, we can easily become micro-managers. We get more and more immersed in the details and can bring week-by-week decision-making by our people to a standstill.

Rather, Senior Executives must get on top of things, literally, and oversee the bigger picture. We need to think in terms of months and quarters and not days and weeks. *Strategists* look into emerging patterns and themes to seek out problems and anticipate challenges. They look at how initiatives and dynamics interconnect with each other to both build forward momentum over time and reduce any drag factors.

And they look at the key milestones to be reached over a three-year plus time horizon to ensure that the pathway designed to arrive at the desired destination is realistic and achievable. Of course the pathway is largely conceptual. A trait of the *Strategist* is to be a trail-blazer, a path-finder. The Strategic Roadmap of Major Milestones provides us with a broad overview. It sets the scene or strategic context within which the work is done from a higher and broader perspective. The actual trail is seen in retrospect.

Greg's Story

Greg was in Sydney to set up the OPAL transit ticketing system. He'd led an equivalent project in Brisbane, Queensland, and Auckland, New Zealand. While successful, both these earlier projects had been delayed by 2-3 years as a result of many unanticipated factors and complex challenges. Here he was again, this time in Sydney, third time lucky! There were around 150 people in his Division plus as many again employed by an external contractor based in London who was developing and delivering the evolutionary new software services to deliver a new $1b+ automated ticketing system called OPAL for Sydney, Australia.

Greg is a tall, kind and cultured man who enjoys the Opera. He is also pragmatic and purposeful, with a genuine appreciation for the customer experience as a boarding passenger. To move beyond being a highly effective leader to becoming an extraordinary leader, Greg wanted to develop greater self-confidence in taking the lead from the front rather than influencing behind the scenes. He also wanted to get out of the detail and develop his people so that they would be able to make sound, robust business decisions.

Greg implemented much of what you will find in this book. His guiding principles were the Customer Value Proposition, Leadership Effectiveness, Internal Collaboration and Project Deliverables in terms of time, cost, safety and quality. If the first three were ably demonstrated, he was confident that the Project Deliverables would be met. This, in and of itself, began to lift his perspective.

While the critical deadlines that had to be met for the program to be successful loomed large in his mind, Greg knew that he could not drive success. He needed to engineer the opportunity for shared success. He had to retain the high ground, the overview, to ensure that the people working with him and his external supplier were empowered and supported to collaborate and innovate as needed to resolve problems as they arose. Only then would they truly succeed.

By taking a bird's eye view of the Major Milestones, Greg was able to see the road ahead and map it out for his people. He appreciated the intricacies of customer conversion, the dynamics within his team and with the external supplier, and the complexities integral in the advanced technology solution. His clear Roadmap and insightful overview meant that his people could take accountability for results and he could coach them to steer around or overcome obstacles and barriers as they emerged.

Over the course of time, his team collaborated more and more. He gave priority to building a sustainable relationship with the external supplier rather than just focusing on contractual compliance. In fact, Greg chose to take a strategic view of the errors and malfunctions that inevitably arose, looking to focus on the source of the problems instead. He traveled to London to develop the business relationship, support their collaborative effort and contribute to resolving problems at cause rather than effect.

Greg also set his aspirational leadership intentions very firmly:

- *My organization is an extension of me – my vision, my voice, my values.*

- *I celebrate the completion of the OPAL Program as Program Director.*

- *I have an enviable reputation for effectively delivering on a $1b+ highly complex program.*

- *I attract an amazing new senior executive opportunity to follow!*

Over time he developed a new level of understanding of himself. About nine months into the coaching program, Greg described his journey as follows:

> *"How I think now is different from before ... Doing the Aspirational Leadership Brand Declaration method of scripting, helped me to be aware of what I've been thinking ... I realized that I was starting the day by saying to myself "I'm tired." I became concerned that this was a bit debilitating ... so I switched it to "I'm ready" during the week leading up to Easter. During this same week I decluttered my desk! I'm also beginning to exercise mindfulness. I'm more aware of what I think, why I think it, what I say, what I do ... Instead of feeling despondent, I feel excited about the day ahead.*

> *I feel like I'm floating a bit as a result of this development I'm doing. It feels as if I was quite attached to what I was doing, and it was all stable, cause and effect and it will happen ... And then to come up that notch, it's like being in water where you can't touch the bottom, I'm still floating, and it's ok, yet I feel nervous sometimes when I can't touch the bottom. Treading water is reinforcing that I'd better get used to this feeling. I'm even enjoying it. It's not a painful process, just disconcerting. I think I've got more energy because of it.*

> *In terms of being authentic, that word resonates with me really strongly, even if I'm feeling a bit fake ... My son's*

friend asked me: 'What do I do?' I said 'I'm a leader of about 400 people', whereas previously I would've offered a really different answer ... I would've described myself as technical expert, project manager or program director, or a leader of a community-wide strategic initiative ... now I'm really seeing myself as a leader of people."

Greg's team managed to meet every single deadline. This was previously unheard of! An amazing accomplishment! By creating a very clear, transparent Strategic Roadmap and engaging his people to take direct responsibility for the results to be achieved, Greg was able to lift his gaze to the personal wellbeing of the people traveling the route and the nature of the path itself. By tuning into their challenges and concerns, he was able to guide them through their dilemmas and develop them as leaders and decision-makers. He was blazing a new trail of collaboration and innovation centered on the passenger experience.

Greg and his people successfully revolutionized the transport ticketing system in NSW on trains, ferries and buses. They have done so with only minor public hiccoughs despite affecting millions of passengers and thousands of operating staff. His higher level perspective tuned into the dynamics of the transformation that was taking place. By exercising foresight and insight he turned what could have been a very disruptive process into an organic, evolving one.

Greg also manifested his breadth of vision by reconstructing his role and enlarging his mandate to redesign the revenue model and amend the approach to ticketing regulation. He now chairs the Committee for Ticketing Revenue Management that includes the CFO and Group General Counsel and has been invited to put together an Intelligent Transport Systems

Strategy. Greg's career has advanced significantly while his personal transformation as a leader from Achiever to Strategist inside the 12-month period was complete.

He reflects:

> *"As a result of our conversations over the year, there are places I've gone to as a leader that I wouldn't have gone to before. I wouldn't be having the conversations with my team today on things that I would have been blind to in the past ... Leadership is a lot of things. One of the things that I've been working on, me tuning into me, has really allowed me not to baulk at these situations. I can now have an open conversation with any one of my team members ... some have been in tears because they are learning things that are fundamental to who they are, developing their own self-awareness.... I'm able to help others become more authentic, authenticity breeds authenticity ... Me growing is causing or generating their growth! I'm empowering them to grow."*

Greg has since been appointed into a new role to lead the management of the OPAL Ticketing System. Needless to say he has a farsighted vision for its opportunity to better serve the explicit and tacit needs of OPAL passengers now and in the future.

A MAJOR MILESTONES ROADMAP

"No problem can be solved from the same level of consciousness that created it. We must learn to see the world anew."
- Albert Einstein

One of the most persistent problems in the workplace is micro-management. This is often the case when an Executive is continuing to operate with the mindset of a *Specialist* requiring everything to be absolutely perfect. The pernicious thing is that once our work has been corrected a few times, it becomes 'normal' to continue to put up 'mostly-done' work knowing that our perfectionist boss will correct anything requiring amendment or adjustment. Often there are simply style differences that the *Specialist* finds difficult to tolerate and this undermines authentic self-expression for team members leading to their disengagement.

Another typical problem is highly controlling behavior when an Executive directs precisely how things must be done. This frequently occurs when your boss and yourself both have an *Achiever* mindset. You want to get from A to B following route X; they prefer route Y. Both are equally valid and effective. If your manager imposes their route, this can become a battle of wills rather than a mutual trust in each person delivering on their responsibilities to ensure that agreed goals are achieved.

Both micro-management, getting caught up in the small stuff, and controlling behavior, driving people to take specific action rather than allowing a performance framework to draw out the best from people, lead to duplication, disengagement, lack of accountability and under-performance. These approaches to management are disempowering. They stymie innovation and creativity. They are manager-centric approaches that impose on people rather than people-centric approaches that encourage individuals to contribute to the best of their ability, develop their talents along the way and make robust, principled decisions that lead to a strong Divisional performance.

Let Go of Micro-Managing and Controlling Behaviors

Further, the strategic work or accountability for the broader strategic context in terms of defining and sequencing a set of strategic initiatives, engaging stakeholders and anticipating community concerns, receive little attention. In many organizations there is such a large proliferation of new initiatives in relation to the internal workings of the organization including software upgrades, new systems and people processes that everyone is put under significant pressure. It seems that no one has taken a view of all the work that has been scheduled by the range of different Divisional managers. They are all setting up their work streams independently of each other to achieve their Divisional performance outcomes regardless of the cumulative impact on the people in the organization.

As a result, everyone is busy, busy, busy trying to achieve numerous things at once. The interconnections between projects and initiatives aren't noticed except by the people at the receiving end who wonder why they must implement

Project C before Initiative A as that means they will need to redo Project C immediately after implementing Initiative A. Without strategic sequencing bottlenecks are commonplace, workforce stress continues to rise and confidence in the Executive Management Team diminishes.

Strategic Sequencing of Key Initiatives Creates Flow

One of the keys to being a really effective strategic leader is to ensure that your people are held accountable for achieving key milestones and delivering the results, in other words, for enacting the performance. A *Strategist* is akin to the conductor of the orchestra or the director of the movie. They play a central and essential role, yet they are not the musicians or actors who actually create the show. They do not themselves produce the performance. Rather they provide the architecture or structure within which individuals and teams achieve the desired performance and they generate the momentum that encourages the effort and initiative to produce the results.

Thus, just as movies and symphonies have critical turning points that lead to a specific experience in the minds and hearts of the audience, it is important to set out the Major Milestones that need to be realized. This ensures a higher perspective or bird's eye view. The Major Milestones Roadmap sets out and communicates the key milestones for the business unit and organization, for all stakeholders and the customers or communities being served. This clarity and transparency facilitate genuine accountability and commitment.

Major Milestones Create Transparent Accountability

The Strategic Roadmap provides an open framework within

which each division, team and person can identify and determine the best actions to take in order to reach the agreed series of intermediary destinations that will ensure successful outcomes. The Roadmap adds the dimension of governance along the route that leads to the achievement of strategic Key Performance Indicators identified in the Transformational Strategic Agenda.

While the Strategic Roadmap documents the key program or project deliverables as Major Milestones, it also documents the Milestones for the Key Strategic Initiatives. These are initiatives that facilitate a strategic shift in performance through systems, processes and technologies or a strategic shift in terms of capacity, capability, collaboration and culture that will enable stronger performance outcomes to be achieved. The selection and sequencing of Key Strategic Initiatives is the responsibility of the Senior Executive leader.

A Key Strategic Initiative by definition is one that will enable the transformational performance and culture shifts to be realized and is designed to directly impact the strategic KPIs. The development of new strategic initiatives requires strategic thinking, foresight and collaboration with stakeholders to create and confirm. This engagement takes place through the course of the monthly Strategic Meetings as part of Orchestrated Stakeholder Engagement – more on this in Chapter 7. Once a Key Strategic Initiative has been agreed, monitoring its progress moves to the fortnightly Operations Meeting.

The creation of a Strategic Roadmap complete with all significant program deliverables and the Major Milestones of key strategic initiatives enables the Executive Leadership Team to see everything that is going to take place over a one to three year time period. This clear oversight enables us to see the bottlenecks, the connections, the disconnects and the incongruities. Only then can the Executive Team as a whole appreciate and determine the ideal order and pace of implementation for each initiative relative to the others to optimize performance and ensure the appropriate resourcing is in place along the way. Viewing new initiatives from the perspective of the people being directly and indirectly affected creates a customer and community-centric focus.

Audience-based Sequencing Creates Customer Focus

Many CEOs labor over the problem that individual Executives restrict their work to their own divisions creating a series of silos in the organization. This is because they are focused only on their own division and do not have any awareness up front on what is happening in other divisions. When there are conflicts, they come up as a surprise. Often Executive Team Meetings focus on how to best resolve these disconnects whereas these issues could all be eliminated upfront through the visibility of a comprehensive Strategic Roadmap.

While the Senior Executive Leader may be the Sponsor for each Strategic Initiative, their Executive Team Members or younger leaders wishing to accelerate their growth, can take up the role of Champion for each Strategic Initiative. These roles also serve to spearhead their development as *Catalysts*. While the CEO, Senior Executive or Director adopting the SOS is on the pathway from *Achiever* to *Catalyst* and onto *Strategist*, it is important to ignite the development of other executives too.

Sponsors and Champions Enable Clear Collaboration

The key challenge for strategic leadership is to see the big picture and to direct and monitor the performance from this perspective. This requires a number of shifts in focus. The first shift in focus is from monitoring activities, to monitoring the achievement of key strategic milestones across all strategic initiatives.

A second is to shift from continuous involvement in decision-making, to entrusting decision-making to the people accountable for achieving the results and focusing instead on building the strategic context to guide robust and aligned decision-making. This can be achieved through the articulation of the strategic shifts and guiding principles. Articulating this strategic context enables aligned, congruent decision-making.

A third strategic accountability is to review all strategic initiatives and their respective milestones on one roadmap such as an excel spreadsheet to optimize sequencing in terms of the order in which each initiative is to be implemented and to ensure an even flow of improvement activities throughout the year.

A fourth advance on this is to appreciate the Strategic Roadmap in relation to the people affected and to synchronize the array of strategic initiatives relative to the different "audiences". This will optimize both effort and impact leading to a more effective flow of work and much improved outcomes.

We Need to Lift Our Focus to See the Big Picture

I experienced the power of setting a Transformational Strategic Agenda in my work as a Management Consultant with a 1,000-person business services organization. My collaboration with the Founding CEO was terrific. As well as being an astute commercial executive, he had great vision and genuine aspirations to create a great culture in his organization.

We launched with the theme: "From Good to Great" measured

by an outstanding customer experience. We built an aspirational Purpose Statement as part of a revised Strategic Agenda and a set of Values based on I CARE: Integrity, Courage, Accountability, Responsiveness and Energy. Our goal was to create an empowering, high performance culture.

We then established a series of Key Strategic Initiatives covering many of the elements you'll find in this book including Team Charters, Leadership Development, Recognition Strategy, revised Performance Management and Values-based Programs with Champions drawn from across the workforce. We rolled them out one after the other based on a Strategic Roadmap that optimized sequencing and resourcing. It was an absolute blast! We built momentum very rapidly through Orchestrated Stakeholder Engagement across the organization. Within 6 months of launch, People Engagement had jumped by 30% due to their successive involvement in the implementation of a concerted synchronized set of Key Strategic Initiatives.

Lift Your People Engagement by 30% in 6 Months

"There will always be rocks in the road ahead of us. They will be stumbling blocks or stepping stones; it all depends on how you use them."
- **Friedrich Nietzche**

KEY IDEAS

1. The role of a Senior Executive is to generate an amazing performance, not to produce it. Setting Major Milestones empowers others to reach those goals while establishing a robust accountability and governance framework. Micro-management and controlling behaviors need to be released.

2. It is important to establish the series of Key Strategic Initiatives to be rolled out in relation to each other with regard to strategic sequencing and the audience. This will streamline work, avoid duplication and build momentum more quickly.

3. Executive governance is optimized by setting key milestones in terms of major events in a concerted way over a period of one to three years based on quarterly projections and the immediate months ahead.

4. Appointing a Champion (Executive Team Member) and Sponsor (Senior Executive) for each strategic initiative ensures that there is an effective collaboration between a driver or change agent (*Achiever* or *Catalyst* respectively) and overseer/mentor/coach (*Catalyst* or *Strategist*).

For more information on Stage Leadership Development, go to www.antoinettebraks/stages

For more information on Executive SOS, go to www.antoinettebraks/SOS

Chapter 4

Create the STYLE

A Values-based Leadership Culture

"Our chief want is someone who will inspire us to be what we know we could be."
- Ralph Waldo Emerson

Mastery of Values

Culture, as we know, is "how we do things around here." The "how" relates to how people connect and engage with each other. When we feel respected and listened to, when we are able to give voice to our authentic views and concerns, and when we are able to work purposefully towards achieving agreed goals, we become engaged. We feel a sense of personal power and the accountability to contribute directly to achieving specific results. This sets up a virtuous circle of trust and confidence in ourselves and the people we work with.

We know from Aon's Best Employer Research amongst others that higher people engagement is correlated to increased business performance. High people engagement coupled with a strong strategic focus on generating great customer and community outcomes generates a high performance culture. Yet many organizations do not focus on creating an engaging culture. They acquiesce to a culture by default.

To shift from a culture by default, one that is the legacy of previous leadership, to a culture by design, one we want, we need to focus on how we exercise our leadership. The culture of an organization is a reflection of how the leaders in that organization operate. Whether they are encouraging and attentive, or discouraging and competitive, either way this filters down as everyone in an organization models their behavior on what they see happening above them.

We each have the power to create an empowering high performance culture around us. The frameworks and processes that you find in Executive SOS are all extremely empowering.

They are designed for people to realize their potential to contribute and grow as leaders rather than diminish their ability to express themselves. However to really create a conversation around the corporate culture, I have found that it is essential to introduce a set of tangible values that communicates the type of behaviors the leaders in an organization wish to encourage.

A transparent set of values give people a frame of reference from which to act. They provide a template of aspirational leadership behaviors that invite us to rise above and resolve interpersonal dynamics in a mature and compassionate way. I have found that they are the ideal vehicle to stimulate leadership development so that rather than react or withdraw, we live into a higher way of being. By becoming more aware of how we operate in relation to an espoused set of values, and paying attention to how to approach situations with respect, integrity and courage, we can create a highly empowering and high performance Values-based Leadership Culture.

Furthermore, we can do this despite the prevailing culture across the organization. If, as an Executive Leader, you choose to introduce a set of Values or give attention to effectively engaging on an existing set of Values, you can create a distinctive culture in your part of the organization. It simply requires you to do three things. First, it's important to orchestrate a concerted approach to values engagement as part of your strategic agenda through the course of monthly cascading Culture meetings; secondly, to invest in your own leadership development so that you develop deeper self-awareness and increase your own leadership capacity; and thirdly, to stand your ground and model the Values in your relationships with your people and colleagues. This will inspire others to do the same.

Jason's Story

Jason is one of the few Executive leaders in government who is Aboriginal. Following a career across a number of departments he now heads up Aboriginal Affairs. The challenge of his position is immense. Aboriginal communities throughout Australia experience significantly worse outcomes than the broader population across a range of indicators, including education, health, incarceration, employment and prosperity.

Efforts to support the Aboriginal communities are spread across multiple departments and tiers of government. They are each charged with goals and targets to improve the wellbeing of the Aboriginal peoples, and all have a series of initiatives targeted to resolve specific issues. However their individual approaches are not well integrated and nor do they have a history of collaborating openly with local Aboriginal communities. The focus has largely been on social services and processes that are supplied rather than open, genuine engagement on their aspirations and concerns.

How do you approach a role that is given the oversight, yet has few resources, little direct influence and is submerged inside a departmental cluster that otherwise has little to do with the cultural, social and economic rights and interests of Aboriginal peoples? Aboriginal Affairs had become something of a bystander, as it did not play an integral role in the shaping of governmental strategies and services across health, education, planning and infrastructure, primary industries, justice and community services. It had largely been relegated to consultative status.

Jason decided to go to the heart of the Aboriginal communities. He first listened to them and then became their Voice into government, the Voice of transformational change and the Voice representing one of the world's oldest continuous cultures. Following deep engagement with Aboriginal communities, he instituted a set of Values that reflected their deepest desires and goals for a better future.

Jason became the Voice for the Values and received substantial recognition and support from amongst the Aboriginal communities. However, within government, he still felt marginalized. He was seen more as a bureaucrat or 'talking head' who would implement and communicate the policies and strategies of the more senior departmental heads across the public sector. Jason wanted to exercise more influence on behalf of the people he represented.

He was also tired of the lack of significant progress over the decades. Jason wanted to close the substantial gaps in economic participation, life expectancy and educational attainment and to resolve persistent land issues, land that is central to the spiritual identity of the Aboriginal peoples. He decided to build a new sense of increased awareness across government, business and society based on the new OCHRE Values.

The Values were beautifully symbolized by the acronym OCHRE, representative of Aboriginal peoples' deep connections to their country. Ochre's cultural significance is reflected in its use in ceremonies to bind people to each other and their country. Ochre is also recognized for its special healing powers promoting physical, emotional and spiritual health.

OCHRE stands for Opportunity, Choice, Healing, Responsibility and Empowerment. These were strong, uplifting, heartfelt values that articulated the great desire for the Aboriginal peoples to become self-governing, to draw pride from their heritage while advancing their culture, and to take charge of their own destiny while letting go of the pain and regrets of the past.

- *With Opportunity, Jason sought to resurrect the Opportunity for Aboriginal Peoples to live strong, meaningful lives congruent with their cultural values.*

- *With Choice, he sought to elevate the concerns of Aboriginal communities so that they could exercise real choice leading to improved outcomes for all.*

- *With Healing, he sought to articulate a new level of understanding and forgiveness to resolve the emotional and spiritual wounds of the past so that the Aboriginal Peoples could heal.*

- *With Responsibility, he sought to support Aboriginal communities take responsibility for their decisions and actions by ensuring that they knew what their options were, collaborated on proposed solutions, exercised community leadership and engaged widely with government.*

- *With Empowerment, he sought to empower Aboriginal Peoples so that they could once again be self-determining and revitalize their language and culture to honor the past and usher in a better future.*

Jason became the Voice for these Values that resonated strongly with Aboriginal communities.

Furthermore, Jason wanted to change the Aboriginal Affairs conversation from gaps, deficits and services, to strengths, expectations and opportunities. Jason believed that, to make a worthwhile difference, he had to focus on a small number of key levers most likely to advance the social, economic and cultural prosperity Aboriginal peoples desired. His strategic choices were to build confidence and leadership capability; to increase economic participation and opportunity; to promote cultural expression and healing; and to broker solutions to complex problems and policy misalignment. All these things were extremely important to Jason.

He started to tune into his own leadership capacity and became more aware when he was backing down and holding himself back from pursuing his strategic agenda. He began to consciously back himself in small ways at first, and later, in relation to major shifts in policy and governance. He learnt the art of saying "No" graciously and courageously in order to be authentic and true to the OCHRE values. Jason gradually extended his sphere of influence as the Voice of the Aboriginal Peoples in government.

He also adjusted his view of the machinations of government. Whereas before he saw all the problems, inconsistencies and bureaucracy, now he looked for the opportunities, pathways and detours he could take. He began to operate in what I call the "orange light zone" where you ask permission of no-one, proceed with care and engage, engage, engage so that people are informed and aware of the strategic direction and progress being made.

As a budding musician, Jason took inspiration from the Beatles hit 'All You Need Is Love':
> 'There's nothing you can do that can't be done
> Nothing you can sing that can't be sung
> Nothing you can say but you can learn how to play the game
> It's easy ...'

And then more change came along. The role of Aboriginal Affairs itself came under review! It seems that Jason's new role *as a strategic advocate had caused those in more senior positions to reconsider the current placement and mandate of Aboriginal Affairs. This led to funding questions that required Jason to put up a new business model and restructure so that he could regain ongoing funding to generate a greater presence in the regional communities.*

Jason was bringing to fruition a shift from a fractured services-based approach that involved multiple disjointed meetings to a community-centric one that brought the OCHRE values to life. He influenced other agendas by taking a community-centric, evidence-based, strategically focused approach orchestrating engagement with government to ensure that innovative phased solutions were implemented effectively. He held the overview rather than being marginalized across the multitude of efforts.

He proposed that Aboriginal Affairs play an integrative role with a whole of community perspective by leading government-to-community governance negotiations to set strategic priorities across health, education, housing, transport, justice and community safety to reflect local priorities and circumstances. He felt that empowerment and genuine power-sharing were the missing elements of previous approaches to Aboriginal Affairs strategy. Creating a level playing field was essential to bring OCHRE to life!

> *Jason reflected: "Who else could do this? No one else has Aboriginal communities at the heart of their purpose. We are the representative voice of Aboriginal communities in government. The Aboriginal communities expect that this is what we're doing.... That's why we need to take the lead. It's all about us ... being empowered ... it's our primary, principal focus."*

Jason took a holiday break and on his return, he found it challenging to settle. While he now had a wonderful Strategic

Agenda and felt purposeful and committed, he simultaneously felt stifled by the endless circle of conversations between Treasury, Ministers and other Departments. He was awake for three nights in a row after returning to work. It seemed so challenging to actually get anything moving! He was sceptical and felt deflated.

This seemed to me to be a passing form of dissonance. Now that Jason had the bit between his teeth, he wanted action. He wanted a shift in attention and to make immediate progress. However this was where the rubber hit the road. This was where he needed to sustain the power of his convictions and drive. Jason reset his Aspirational Leadership Brand Declaration, as "I am a bold and innovative leader".

Then he started to see more progress. He detached himself further from the drama and noise, and began to give greater Voice to his agenda tying key change initiatives to OCHRE. Jason began to advance his Strategic Platform by giving Voice to asking for more investment for a long enough period of time to remedy the trauma and underlying causes rather than service the symptoms of Aboriginal disadvantage.

> *"Our next big thing is to create two way conversations, empower people, generate engagement from the inside out, where local communities become self-determining and get the service and employment they need, strong and united."*

Jason ended up getting support for his new role, operating model and structure he proposed for Aboriginal Affairs and a layer of management above him was removed. By exception, he also obtained an extension to fixed term funding with an agreed process and timeframe for revisiting his bid for permanent funding.

> *"We are still getting things done. Three years of hard*

work and negotiation culminated with the tabling of a Bill of significant Land Rights Act amendments in Parliament a fortnight ago, while last week we released the latest OCHRE Report highlighting achievements over the first 12 months of implementation."

Jason's opening paragraph in the First Annual OCHRE Report:

"Reflecting on the past year, one of the most encouraging trends has been the overwhelmingly positive response from Aboriginal communities. OCHRE is, at its heart, a strong plan with clearly focused goals that follows a life course approach to achieve enduring, generational change. Throughout this first year of its implementation, we have emphasized a genuine, ongoing, two-way dialogue with Aboriginal communities to ensure everybody is on the journey together. This has given Aboriginal communities a strong sense of ownership and has given us the confidence to stand behind the commitments made within OCHRE."

Njunaliin ngaralanga dharawalwulawala nguradhanhay ngaliya

[We respect Aboriginal peoples as the first peoples and custodians of NSW]

A VALUES-BASED
LEADERSHIP CULTURE

"Try not to become a man of success.
Rather become a man of value."
- Albert Einstein

Values bring us to the heart of things. While strategic goals are essential in terms of mindful endeavor, they don't go to the core of relationship concerns or community spirit. Values provide us with a sense of identity, an appreciation of personal growth and the opportunity to be our best selves. Talking about Values gives us license to have conversations that we would otherwise avoid. It gives us permission to be the whistleblower on disrespectful behavior, which, in some way, will undoubtedly transgress a shared Value.

Values travel up the spiral of leadership development. There are positive values at each leadership stage. For instance, at the level of *Specialist*, values such as quality and excellence are important. At the *Achiever* level, customers, results and accountability come into focus. At the *Catalyst* level we see authenticity, courage, and innovation as we learn to appreciate our own conscious self-expression from the inside-out. And at *Strategist*, we value transformation, trust, collaboration, sustainability and the advancement of 'whole of community' interests.

Ideally your set of values includes qualities or ideals from a range of the leadership stages and includes some aspirational values to live up to. Indeed values in and of themselves catapult us into the realm of the *Catalyst*. While the *Specialist* focuses on their work or their craft, and *Achievers* focus on their goals, it is only at *Catalyst* level that we begin to explore within. This inner exploration includes ascertaining our values, motivations and concerns, and discerning the messages offered to us by our emotions and intuition. Thus establishing a Values-based Leadership Culture in and of itself sets up the opportunity for leadership development.

Aspirational Values Aid Stage Development to *Catalyst*

Another way to ensure you create a balanced set of values is to check for a spread across the four dimensions of Being: Doing, Relating, Thinking and Creating or AQ, Action Orientation; EQ, Emotional Awareness; MQ Mindful Attention; and SQ, Spiritual Intelligence. If a whole dimension is missing, it will create a blind spot in your Values engagement and in your Leadership Model if it is also based on your Values.

By combining and integrating various capabilities around a Value, you can create your own Values-based Leadership Model. This is an ideal way to define the Values and describe relevant leadership behaviors at each broad role level within the organization from the psychological perspective of Stage Leadership Development.

In the Holistic Leadership Model, the foundational level of behaviors is described at the *Specialist* level – called Self. The next level of *Achiever* is correlated with the role of Manager – a Project Manager, Team Leader or Business Unit Manager. The stage of *Catalyst* is designated Leader, representing roles such as Functional, Commercial and Divisional Heads, Program Directors and any senior roles that roam across the organization or extend widely outside the organization. The stage of *Strategist* is for C-suite roles and *Alchemist* for the likes of Corporate Presidents and Directors-General. After working with a fashion brand, we found it fun and simple to use the initials S, M, L, XL and XXL to designate these progressive role levels – Self, Manager, Leader, Executive Leader and Senior Executive Leader!!

Create a Values-based Stage-centric Leadership Model

A most efficient and effective way to roll out Values in an organization is to center the Culture component of the Strategic Agenda each month around one Value at a time over a 2-3 month time period. This enables meaningful conversation to take place within teams and across divisions. By creating a process that includes reflection and alignment, engagement and development, the organization's culture can rapidly become a culture by design rather than by default.

One of the most underused yet highly cost-effective methods to stimulate cultural renewal is a Values-based Recognition Strategy. This ensures that consistent attention is given to the demonstration of core Values thereby rewarding leadership development and ensuring that success stories are celebrated and shared. Actually giving regard to an individual's or team's kind deed, special endeavor or amazing success that made a big difference to someone or a group of people inside or outside the organization, in a heartfelt way, brings smiles to everyone's faces and tears to a few. There are many ways Recognition can bring Values to life with tangible products, certificates and annual live events to celebrate the best of the best!

As bold words on colorful wall posters, the Values remind us what to pay attention to; as taglines on our email signatures they define our promise to the outside world; as the foundational structure for a leadership model they advance Stage Leadership Development; and enshrined in a Recognition Strategy, they celebrate our best qualities and most magical moments. As they are lived and breathed, Values become meaningful on a deeply personal level and have the power to completely transform your culture quickly and easily.

Values Come Alive In Culture Meetings and Recognition

In addition to the above creative strategies, the trick is also to inhibit the old culture by overcoming complacency. Complacency is endemic. It's easier to carry on behaving the same way as yesterday than to assume a conscious witness perspective on how we are operating day by day, spending our time, treating others and making our lives worthy of being lived. Yet this is precisely the point of living: to live more powerful, positive and purposeful lives. This enables us to evolve and develop the wisdom and compassion of great leaders who have learnt to demonstrate personal mastery.

We can only overcome complacency by setting and maintaining standards, boundaries and priorities. This leads to the formation of new habits. At first I thought these were the mark of a high *Achiever* but, through the course of Executive Coaching, I found that only *Strategists* held their standards, boundaries and priorities rigorously and definitively. They truly 'walk their talk'. During any discourse on a particular Value, standards, boundaries and priorities can be discerned and better understood.

To 'walk the talk', you, the leader, must be a whistle blower. To be a whistle blower is to call out inappropriate behavior, and particularly behavior that does not meet the standards set for a corporate Value. It is critical that this is done in every single instance as only then does everyone start to take the Values seriously. As soon as a transgression is overlooked, the momentum to create the new culture is lost. Of course if Senior Executive leaders do not maintain the new standards, neither will anyone else. However you do have the power to hold them for your Division.

Often an opportunity presents itself to create a dramatic turning point. It's as if the old culture meets the new culture in a standoff. Who will win? This is the time to create a dramatic watershed event that everyone will talk about and remember. You may have read of instances when a new leader gathered all the old policy documents together into a pile in the car park and set them alight. Or when the CEO required one of the most Senior Executives to attend a training course on non-bullying behavior. Or when one of the highest performing salespeople was invited to move on if they couldn't apologize to their colleagues.

To Live the Values We Must Become Whistle-Blowers

I can still recall the tremors in my throat, the rapid pace of my heartbeat and the agitation that seemed to stir within every single cell of my body when I was faced with a personal values challenge. I was having a conversation with a CEO and risking my entire consulting assignment by disagreeing with him and not backing down. I couldn't even believe I was doing it. I had left two other assignments in the previous three months due to what I perceived as a lack of integrity in the people around me. And I felt so fortunate to have won this assignment in the midst of the GFC. Plus I was loving the work. Now I was putting it all at risk. That night I wondered to myself, "Was the issue really so important to put my economic stability in danger – yet again?!"

The next day I did expect to be fired. I couldn't believe I had put my own financial wellbeing at risk when I could've found a way to come to an agreement. However we had launched a set of values including Courage and Integrity. I had to be true to myself given that I was leading the Cultural Transformation. Surprisingly to me, it turned out that the CEO's respect for me increased. Suddenly it seemed I was a person prepared to stand their ground and even more astounding to me at the time, other people noticed the subtle shift in the relationship. I learned that slight changes in relationship dynamics are very apparent to others. It is moments like this that forge character and create a tangible shift in culture!

Culture matters. It is impossible to sustain a high performance organization unless there is a strong and distinctive, positive, empowering culture. A high performance culture embraces people's strengths, their potential for personal growth and their mutual regard and respect for one another as members of a community. A shift to a mutually beneficial and mutually respectful culture automatically leads to higher engagement and increased wellbeing.

"Your beliefs become your thoughts, Your thoughts become your words,
Your words become your actions, Your actions become your habits,
Your habits become your values, Your values become your destiny."
- Mahatma Gandhi

KEY IDEAS

1. Create a culture by design based on a strategically selected set of Values having regard to balance across Doing, Thinking, Relating and Creating, and to Stages of Leadership.

2. Bring the Values to life through strategic Culture engagement, continuing leadership development, a powerful recognition strategy and vibrant frequent internal communications.

3. Hold high standards and strong boundaries and be on the alert for whistle blowing opportunities to create a dramatic watershed event of a standoff with the old culture, both personally and in respect of the behavior of others.

4. A Values-based Leadership Culture embraces people, growth and community outcomes leading to increased engagement, performance and wellbeing.

For more information on Stage Leadership Development, go to www.antoinettebraks/stages

For more information on Executive SOS, go to www.antoinettebraks/SOS

Chapter 5

Know the SCORE

Cascading Team Charters

"Talent wins games, but teamwork and intelligence wins championships."
- Michael Jordan

Mastery of Teamwork

Knowing the SCORE puts you ahead of the game. First, it gives you a feedback loop. By checking the SCORE, you know if your chosen activities are producing the desired results. This is an essential element of the organizational infrastructure if people are to shift from the mindset of a *Specialist* focused inwardly on their work to the mindset of an *Achiever* focused outwardly on their customer. This empowers your people to make decisions aligned with the achievement of better results rather than relying on your approvals and permissions.

Secondly, setting targets against specific measures opens up the Energy Field of 'Creative Stretch' held together by Desire and a Vision of the future. As soon as we enter this Energy Field life becomes easier and more fluid than when we were anchored in a mindset below that of *Achiever*. Rather than life going up and down in 'Reactive Patterns' as it does for *Conformists*, we enter the playground of "stretch and grow". We take more steps forward than we do backwards. We make progress. We are comfortable taking measured risks and move into our growth zone to learn how to become increasingly more effective and efficient!

Thirdly, the SCORE focuses on Team Results. Rather than maximizing each individual's contribution individually we focus on how to optimize each person's individual contribution to generate the best team performance. This is still outside of the norm in many organizations where people management is only based on a review of their performance in relation to their individual position description or performance agreement. The shift to team performance will make a significant difference to engaging and empowering individuals to inspire high team performance.

Finally Cascading Team Charters enable you to cascade the Transformational Strategic Agenda and Major Milestones Roadmap as well as the Values-based Leadership Culture throughout your organization or division. The Team Charter cascades data from the Executive Leadership Team and applies and interprets it to each role level and type of work. You'll be able to orchestrate the strategic focus of your people in such a way that you really are conducting the orchestra and everyone is playing from the same song-sheet or musical SCORE! The Dynamic Diary Rhythm keeps everyone in time through the course of the year.

Kate's Story

Kate was a kind and highly effective leader renown for her astute intelligence and valued for her pragmatic approach. However, as a female scientist in a very male dominated world, she had always found it challenging to assert her own authority. With a slight build, a soft, sometimes tenuous voice and quiet demeanor, she didn't immediately come across as highly confident. Kate also felt a little uncomfortable amongst people she didn't know and was not at ease networking. She was clearly capable yet understated. Kate was also respectful of those in authority and did not really recognize the great respect others held for her.

She had successfully shifted from the worldview of the Specialist as a scientist, to become anchored as an Achiever. She was focused on project deliverables, value creation and community outcomes based on scientific research. She had recently taken up a new role to lead Science within the Office of the Environment and Heritage. Science was critical to the effective stewardship of the environment particularly in the context of a hungry resources industry. Kate believed that Science could make a significant impact by putting powerful facts on the table not colored by prejudice or opinion to better meet the needs of all stakeholders: industry, the wider community and the environment itself.

Previously Science had been a service provider gauging, tracking and reporting changes in air quality, water quality, the diversity of bird and animal life. The Division had been more of an operational unit than a strategic contributor. Her team of scientists had been largely fulfilling their duties with eyes focused on the microscope rather than the telescope. This Kate was determined to change. While the scientific evidence was essential to monitor the environment, it was even more valuable for strategic decision making in relation to environmental impact.

Kate was charged with resetting strategic direction and restructuring her division while reducing employee numbers. She developed a new structure removing duplication and aligning teams around areas of value creation with greater responsibility for evidence-based strategy development. She wanted the Science Division to be an integral part of the Office of the Environment and Heritage so that decisions were made strategically in the light of economic, environmental and community goals and concerns.

She also took great care on the configuration of the roles in her executive team in order to be able to appoint a set of people with a balanced mix of wide-ranging talents. Kate wanted to ensure that she did not recruit in her own likeness and that a diversity of styles and strengths would be present in her team. She made a series of appointments including both experienced employees and newcomers to forge a strong new management team.

Following her restructure one of the first things Kate embarked on was the development of a Team Charter with her Executive Team. We all got together for a day and developed a rich Strategic Agenda including a Purpose Statement: 'SCIENCE for a healthy and vibrant environment that sustains and enriches life in NSW', a Vision of the future based on a clear set of Key Strategic Outcomes that encapsulated Strategic Shifts in Performance and Culture including measures, benchmarks and targets over a 3-year period with a view of optimal end results 7 years hence.

These quantitative goals were supported by Key Strategic Initiatives beyond business-as-usual that would transform the current way of doing business to an entirely new level of operating. Leadership, Excellence and Valued Partnerships were selected as the key guiding principles. They informed the Strategic Framework for the SCORE or Scorecard, to monitor divisional performance and indeed inform organizational performance on many of the same shared indicators.

In the afternoon we reviewed the results of a Team Leadership Culture Survey and created a new set of Values to mark the desired shift in culture. The acronym CREATE standing for Collaboration, Relevance, Exploration, Accessibility, Teamwork and Excellence, emerged to underpin a Values-based Stage-centric Leadership Model. Finally, at the end of the day, we instigated an agreed Dynamic Diary Rhythm and a few other operating norms to generate collaborative teamwork.

In her own time Kate also carefully developed a variety of personal Aspirational Leadership Brand Declarations to embody her own leadership potential. They were a genuine way to articulate her closely held desires and true aspirations.

- *I am bold and brave as an innovative leader of Science*

- *I am dedicated and persist with courageous new initiatives*

- *I collaborate with colleagues and trust and support all the people in Science to contribute, achieve and grow*

- *I relish intellectual and philosophical dialogue and enjoy inquiring into the rationale for the role Science is playing in the world*

- *I delight in seeing the work of others contribute to the wider vision*

- *I am kind, clear thinking and value my integrity*
- *I express myself articulately, authentically and eloquently*
- *I challenge paradigms and bring forth renewal and evolutionary change*

Later, she added:

- *I am a globally recognized strategic leader pursuing the salience of Science in the community.*

All of these statements focused on encouragement, engagement, eloquence, enjoyment and evolutionary change reflected Kate's aspirations to shift her leadership capacity to that of a Catalyst/Strategist.

Her systematic, strategic and scientific approach to confidently implementing the new SOS architecture step-by-step through to Cascading Team Charters throughout her Division enabled her to manifest her strategic perspective. She shifted the goal posts to ignite strong leadership across her management team, led the development of a high performing culture, and then exercised strategic leadership across the organization by reporting widely against their Strategic Agenda.

Furthermore her follow through in terms of cyclical engagement throughout the year across the Science Division of 150 people spread geographically, consolidated the transformational role Science would take. This was not just one workshop for the executives at the top but a series of employee workshops over time that built significant momentum and turned the tide towards creating the future. In a word, they were "humming".

A factor in Kate's transformation was that the newly formed Office of the Environment and Heritage was still finding its place in the world and if anything, had a low political and public profile. By taking the lead at her level as a member of the Senior Executive Team, Kate was able to ignite an empowering strategic direction for her Division.

A newly appointed CEO told Kate that it would be "devastating for OEH to lose the Science Division". Kate's Strategic Agenda had indeed built integrated partnerships across the Division and united them. She had accomplished precisely what she set out to do as a bold and brave innovative leader of Science exercising courage and discipline to bring forth strategic renewal and evolutionary change!

Her final Stage Leadership Assessment Result placed her on the border of Strategist from the position of Achiever a year previously. Her capacity to generate and hold transformation was evident in her personal development as a visionary leader who inspired others and ignited the transformation of not only her division, but her organization as a whole. Kate's emergence as an eminent leader was testimony to the aspirational and far-reaching nature of her Strategic Agenda and orchestrated effect of Cascading Team Charters. They created alignment, congruence and coherence for everyone.

As Kate explained:

> *"We've now got a clear and visionary direction for the Science Division. The big picture is comprehensible and meaningful. It helps us know what to do and conveys ownership of the outcomes for all of the people in Science. It's tangible as well, we all understand it and own it.*

> *My next focus is outward. I would like to expand the voice of Science in Government. I'd like Science to be more influential so that decisions are made with full consideration of up-to-date rigorous science. We need to balance social values and economic goals. And we*

need everyone to become more environmentally literate so that there is greater community awareness and participation in preserving and creating a healthy environment to support healthy living."

CASCADING TEAM CHARTERS

"Oh the places to go! There is fun to be done!
There are points to be scored. There are games to be won.
And the magical things you can do with that ball
Will make you the winning-est winner of all."
- Dr. Seuss

Your Transformational Strategic Agenda enables you to play your role as *Catalysts* and *Strategists*. It sets the overall purpose and key performance outcomes in terms of quantitative targets that will demonstrate that your aspirational vision has been realized. When the purpose, guiding principles, strategic shifts and performance targets are cascaded throughout the organization by way of Team Charters, the entire focus of the organization is unified and uplifted.

The Team Charter is the vehicle that cascades the strategic performance and culture shifts right through the organization. It carries the empowering architecture to each team at their level of operation and creates a focus on shared team results to generate a high performance culture. It also includes the Values and the chosen Dynamic Diary Rhythm to create a unified accord. Cascading Team Charters provide the strategic scaffolding for all members of the organization to become *Achievers*.

The Team Charter for each team is ideally developed during the course of a one-day Strategic Offsite, following a two-day Strategic Offsite for the originating Executive Leadership Team. The focus is on open engagement to apply and interpret the strategic direction set a level above. It is therefore an empowering process that leads to new insights and initiatives, and concerted action over the course of the rest of the year.

Keeping SCORE provides every team with a feedback loop on the extent to which their activities are producing the desired results. When people are focused on results, they can develop as leaders and shift from the more limiting mindsets of *Conformists* and *Specialists* to develop the creative mindsets of strong *Achievers*. The cascading Key Performance Indicators ensure alignment across the organization while the monthly results provide the essential feedback loop on the effectiveness of the particular mix and quality of activities in the previous period.

Cascading Team Charters Uplift People to *Achievers*

Take a moment to imagine an orchestra seated before you. It is made up of various sections, the woodwind instruments, percussion, strings, brass and keyboard section, just as an organization is made up of various divisions. In an orchestra they all play to the same musical composition. They are, as it were, on song being held in accord with the conductor's baton! While the SCORE is intended to represent the Scorecard of KPIs including outcomes, measures, targets and results, an integrated series of scorecards can also be seen as a musical score that keeps everyone on song.

The individual instrumentalists practice beforehand, then rehearse together to finally grant their eager audience a polished performance. Imagine if your organization or division were on the same song sheet! As the conductor, you would simply need to lift and elegantly swing your baton to keep everyone in time. Indeed the conductor of the orchestra is a great analogy for an executive leader operating as a *Strategist*. Everyone is orchestrated, all playing the same symphony with their own unique voice, feeling empowered, liberated and swept up by the rhapsody of the music itself.

The cascading Team Performance Charters combined form a synchronized song sheet. They give people an immediate reference point regarding their strategic and operational goals. The Purpose and Values also contained in the Charter bring spirit and heart into play to direct the style and tone with which actions are taken. And the Dynamic Diary Rhythm keeps everyone in synch!

The Musical SCORE Keeps Everyone In Synch and On Song

Indeed the Team Charter Rollout lifts the Executive Team's Performance to that of the CEO; it lifts the Management Team Performances to that of the Executives; and Team Performances to that required by their Manager. As soon as Transformational Strategic Leadership is genuinely exercised at the top, the Team Charter Cascade lifts the whole organization, level by level.

This is a relevant time to talk briefly about organizational levels. There are generally far too many levels in most organizations with countless small teams of two to four people, and role bands that are narrow in definition. It is much more empowering for teams to consist of seven, plus or minus two, in other words between five and nine where the great majority of teams are seven-a-side.

If there are 7+/-2 people in teams across an organization, the rollout of Team Charters can run smoothly. If there are far too many teams, you may wish to restructure first. Then you will need to collapse role gradings into broad role bands. This allows for a much broader field of appointments across a broader role level, thereby also flattening the organizational structure and facilitating stretch roles for entrants and mentoring type roles for seniors within each band.

Lift The Performance of Teams with 7 +/- 2 a Side!

It also helps to delineate the level of the role with the relevant stage of leadership. It is highly valuable if the person at the top is firmly anchored as a *Strategist*. This will lift the entire organization. The *Catalyst* mindset is very valuable for members of the Executive Team and especially in roles that cut across the divisions of the organization. The *Catalyst* is comfortable and confident engaging across boundaries.

All line management roles are ideally filled by *Achievers*. *Achievers* focus on results, they enjoy teamwork and are decisive, confident, pragmatic and proactive. They will happily co-create a plan of action and keep everyone's eyes focused on the desired outcomes. The Nike catch phrase "Let's do it" is symbolic of the *Achiever*.

Specialists are better with the detail. They will ensure that all activities are carried out to the relevant quality standard. They will focus on the continuous incremental improvement of processes to ensure greater efficiency next time round. The shadow side of the Specialist is to get mired in the detail and become "stuck in the mud." If their leader is an *Achiever*, it will help them enormously to set priorities and ensure quality is fit for purpose rather than absolutely perfect.

The two early stages of leadership development, *Opportunist* and *Conformist*, are redundant in a high performing organization. While we need to bring the positive aspects of these stages to later stages – this is the holarchic nature of the Stage Leadership model where each stage includes the positive qualities of those prior – the shadow or negative passive-aggressive dynamics of these mindsets will sabotage the team and organization.

Further, by identifying the level of Stage Leadership that is most relevant to the level of role, it is also possible to create leadership-developmental career paths for Specialists, Managers, Leaders and Executive Leaders (S, M, L, XL and XXL). Well-devised career paths enable executives to progressively evolve along the pathway from *Specialists* to *Achievers*, *Catalysts* and *Strategists*. Once people consolidate in a stage, they will need a different type of role to develop their leadership capacity further.

Match the Role Level with the Relevant Leadership Stage

Teams can run as baseball or basketball teams. As baseball teams, each individual player plays their position at bat one at a time, and then fields as a unit although still holding their particular places on the field. As a basketball team, each individual player plays the whole court consistently moving back and forth from attack to defense based on the situation. The more basketball you play, the more dynamic and nimble the team.

Whether you are playing baseball or basketball, it is critical that each person's strengths match the critical capabilities they need to be successful in their role. This is often configured as a highly complicated process of matching the level of competence of a person with the requirements of a role. However this does not go to the nature of the role nor the intrinsic talents of the individual.

A much simpler organic approach to strengths matching is to define both roles and people as two principal dimensions from amongst the four ways of being: Doing, Relating, Thinking and Creating (AQ, EQ, MQ and SQ respectively). Generally speaking most people have two primary preferences e.g. a Thinker/Doer or a Creator/Relater. Imagine that we each hold a hand of ten playing cards. The predominant suits are our preferences and it is our natural inclination to play our own best hand and develop those strengths first.

Match Strengths and Preferences to the Nature of the Role

If a person's preferences match the nature of the role, they will enjoy their work and perform well. If they do not, there is nothing you can actually do to facilitate high performance. It is simply not appropriate for a person to carry out work that does not match the type of work they love to do. Indeed these situations create blind spots in organizations that lead to significant performance risk. The only exception to this is at *Catalyst* stage when it could be very timely to bring the person's third suit into play.

By matching both strengths (AQ, EQ, MQ and SQ) and stage (S, M, L, XL, XXL) using the Holistic Leadership Model, you will be able to ensure that there is both spread and stretch across all members of the team. If the work requires some creativity, you will need a couple of Creatives on your team. If the work requires close attention to detail, you will need Thinkers on your team. The more senior the team and the broader the spread of preferences or, in other words, the greater the diversity of strengths, the stronger the team.

The SCORE integrates results and outcomes with teamwork and talent. It's not about how much we do or deliver, it's all about taking accountability for the effect or impact we have on the people we serve, today's customers, the broader community and future generations. The transparent visibility of a Team Scorecard and the resounding alignment of a musical SCORE orchestrating the organization's efforts and initiatives, leads to increasingly high performance. Our human potential to create our future comes alive.

Link Results and Responsibility with Teamwork and Talent

"Teamwork is the ability to work together toward a common vision. The ability to direct individual accomplishments toward organizational objectives. It is the fuel that allows common people to attain uncommon results."
- Andrew Carnegie

KEY IDEAS

1. Cascading Team Charters with a Scorecard of KPIs has the power to lift everyone to the Stage Leadership capacity of an *Achiever*.

2. The development of broad role bands and teams of 7+/-2 has the effect of flattening the organization and empowering team performance.

3. High team performance enshrines individual talents and preferences to optimize the whole and leads to playing the fluid game of basketball instead of the more positional play in baseball.

4. Cascading Strategic and Culture Meeting Agendas throughout Team Meetings during the same week orchestrates attention, alignment and activity, and creates a sense of community.

For more information on Stage Leadership Development, go to
www.antoinettebraks/stages

For more information on Executive SOS, go to www.antoinettebraks/SOS

Chapter 6

Step Up On STAGE

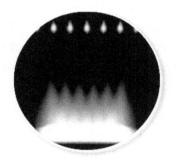

A Compelling Signature Presentation

"Our lives begin to end the day we become silent about things that matter."
- Martin Luther King Jr

Mastery of Voice

One of the key challenges as a Senior Executive with responsibility for visionary leadership is to find and articulate our authentic Voice. We must do this in a variety of ways from a short debrief or update, a challenging conversation with someone with a different perspective, a presentation to a forum of colleagues or stakeholders to persuade them of the importance of whatever it is we hold dear, to leading an open structured dialogue amongst high level decision-makers to generate open engagement, strategic alignment and community coherence.

This is a serious step-up from providing information and reporting progress. Rather than just informing others we seek to influence them to a specific point of view while also reconsidering our perspective in the light of their concerns and wishes. This requires that we articulate our perspective coherently and sincerely, being as authentic as possible to give Voice to our individual self-expression, while advocating a shift in paradigms that enable others to better understand our point of view.

To exercise courageous authenticity is to speak our truth with conviction and candor. This truth includes a visionary view of the future, one that mirrors our highest aspirations for ourselves, our organization and the people we serve. We need to be bold and brave in the face of cynicism and derision, something we must expect and acknowledge as a reflection of others' fears. Simultaneously we must have an open heart to bring others with us. Our language needs to encompass our audience, their needs, concerns, goals and aspirations. The greater our authenticity and commitment and the better we tune into the audience, the more inspiring and convincing we will be.

John's Story

John is a tall, thoughtful person who is relatively shy and genuinely sincere. He is diligent and dedicated to his work leading a Safety Improvement Program in the rail industry. While he cared enormously for his colleagues, John was hesitant around people and did not consider himself good at building relationships.

That said, he was highly effective in his role. High-risk incidents had dropped by 70% in the first three years of the Program. The primary focus was Zero Incidents and ensuring all workers got home safe each day.

John had three strong strategic themes in place: coaching and mentoring the people on the front line working on the track; reviewing work processes and practices to ensure that safety was integral to the way work was carried out; and adopting new tools and technologies to support the track workers. These themes were underpinned by engaging stakeholders across the whole industry and using robust data to assist in decision-making.

However John and his organization were at a turning point. A major restructure was taking place and over 300 senior roles were to be advertised. The size and scope of the reform agenda was substantial. Across the organization there was a significant amount of distraction, concern, uncertainty, negativity, anger and resentment that accompanied the change. Colleagues who had worked alongside each other for many years were leaving and many new people were arriving.

Apart from the harmful effect this could have on the safety culture, John was also concerned if he would personally retain his role or not. While he was approaching retirement, he really wanted to continue his work there. John expressed his goals as:

> *"I would like to operate differently ... I would like to be more confident ... I need to get more strategic.... I need to identify and take the opportunities that always accompany change."*

John developed his Aspirational Leadership Brand Declaration in the following words:

- *I am a man of integrity; I enjoy life with family and friends; and I make a positive difference to the lives of others.*
- *I treat everyone fairly and respectfully. I support my children to be good citizens and to fulfill their potential and there is mutual respect across the family.*
- *I support colleagues to succeed in their careers and fulfill their potential. I consult widely and am recognized as a genuine Safety Change Champion.*
- *I am financially secure. I maintain a positive attitude, and a healthy mind and body. I develop a new skill every year and actively enjoy the outdoors and restoring old cars.*
- *I am an informed and insightful contributor to discussions, learn from any mistakes and continuously raise my self-awareness. I use resources wisely and make a significant contribution to the community.*

John distilled this into a short, memorable intention that he could bring to mind effortlessly at any moment of the day.

> *"I am a man of integrity and I am a confident leader."*

A few months later John advised:

> *"My conscience is on the lookout for me when I do not*

act with genuine integrity."

Setting up commitments like this with the powers of conscious intention and attention facilitates leadership development because in doing so we invite the development of the leadership qualities we attest to.

John wanted to demonstrate his confidence through authentic, authoritative and persuasive communication skills. Like many executives, he was unaccustomed to speaking openly, to proactively sharing his Vision and engaging his colleagues with purpose and conviction. The common thread in John's coaching program was the development of communication strategies to address critical situations and take up opportunities to lead from a strategic perspective.

The first challenge that arose was his need to present effectively at a weekly stand-up meeting where executives had just 5 minutes to update their colleagues. John was always up first and had been feeling quite apprehensive in the face of criticism. The 3 P's put paid to that. A brief point on each of Progress, Problems and Priorities streamlined his communication into a punchy, clear and concise presentation that others began to emulate.

The second challenge is one faced by all Executives. How do you have that conversation you need to have with someone but don't really want to have it? You feel the need to give them some constructive feedback or to assert your point of view when you know it differs from theirs. Or they need to change their behavior or attitude in some way because it's adversely affecting other people. You're not sure how they're going to react yet you know you must say something to resolve the situation.

I call this a Courageous Caring Conversation. The TIP formula includes speaking your Truth, explaining the Implications and arriving at a Point – a turning point in the form of a decision that you have decided to take or action(s) that they must take or put a stop to. Implicit in the formula is the need to stay on message, pause to enable the other person to respond, and to speak with an open mind and an open heart. John learnt how to prepare his thoughts and refine his words to speak up kindly and clearly.

The third opportunity to position himself as a strong, confident leader emerged during the formation of a new national forum to promote the safety of track workers. He was one of three conveners to speak at the initial meeting and it was important for him to present well. We developed a great opening statement that focused on his Principles, Perspective and Purpose.

> *"Hi everyone, I'm John. I currently lead a Safety Improvement Program where we have reduced serious incidents by 70% over 3 years by following three key <u>Principles</u>.*
> *1 Taking a coaching and mentoring approach with frontline track workers*
> *2 Engaging widely with stakeholders including unions and contractors*
> *3 Collecting data and ensuring data integrity to support robust decision-making*
>
> *<u>Perspective</u>*
> *I think we're in a much better place than we used to be as an industry. We've made huge improvements in terms of people staying safe, but we can still improve further. For instance, in an even higher risk industry such as ... their safety record is amazing. They have ...*
>
> *<u>Purpose</u>*
> *In this forum I would like for us to build relationships,*

*carry out benchmarking, share experiences, and learn
from each other to lift our game as an industry so that
we can achieve really excellent safety outcomes."*

This introduction was both strategic and sincere. He voiced the
things that were important, inspiring and meaningful to him.

Later John was invited to speak in a large auditorium filled with
over 1,000 construction workers. While he was nervous, John
was also confident! He made an engaging presentation using
video clips of real events illustrating the danger of operating
without exercising vigilance for personal safety and the safety
of co-workers.

You can see that John was really developing his leadership
presence. He was taking huge strides forward. Opportunities
seem to find us when we prepare ourselves for them!

John remained in his role and his team was largely untouched
through the restructure. He was actively putting himself and his
message forward in the spirit of being of service to others. The
Safety Improvement Program was then moved out of the
operating group where it had been established and into the
Corporate Safety Group. This reflected the truly strategic role
that the Program was to adopt across the whole organization!

At this point John's confidence blossomed. He decided to
construct a 5-year Strategic Agenda that integrated all the
elements described in the previous chapters. John distilled this
into a single page (A3) showing in a simple way how each
Strategic Principle and Strategic Theme, each Set of Measures
and Set of Initiatives, were aligned with the organization's five
Values.

And yes, he then received another invitation to present!!! This
time it was to take place over the course of a half-day workshop
with a group of the most Senior Executives including the CEO.

John had built his Strategic Agenda above around a new Purpose: "Everyone Safe Everyday". He was able to present his pitch bit-by-bit inviting group engagement to amend and refine his team's work during the afternoon. The workshop was a great success and a tribute to John's strategic leadership.

There was just one more thing that empowered John to become an even more confident and inspiring leader. We collaborated on creating his Compelling Signature Presentation – the full 12 P's that enable us to develop a unique and distinctive strategic stage presence while inspiring, persuading and convincing others!!

One of my favorite comments from John is:

> *"I always looked forward to my coaching sessions with Antoinette, however was never sure what new challenges she would be coming up with for me. I would always leave with my head spinning, thinking wow, this will be great ..."*

A COMPELLING SIGNATURE PRESENTATION

"All the world's a stage, and all the men and women merely players.
They have their exits and their entrances ..."
- William Shakespeare

When I was attending a Conference a few years ago, I was very excited about listening to one of the keynote presenters. I had heard their presentation some years ago and found it inspiring and invigorating. As I was listening to them speak, I discovered that it was virtually the same presentation they had given the last time I had heard them, and it was still just as riveting! A few of the case studies had changed and their ideas had evolved, but the same key messages came across eloquently and convincingly! The more we express our authentic voice, the more we learn to know ourselves and appreciate the strategic context within which we are voicing our views. This expanded awareness enables us to become increasingly persuasive and inspiring.

It made me realize that once we have discovered our true purpose and passion, we could create a Compelling Signature Presentation that would express our Voice in the world. That Signature Presentation could be used as a whole, in parts to address specific topics or audiences, or in short form to summarize our perspective. By articulating our authentic Voice, we could build on our key messages over time, with greater subtlety and sincerity with each passing year. In this way we can become truly aligned with our life purpose.

The sixth step to becoming an inspiring strategic leader at *Strategist* level is the ongoing development of a Compelling Signature Presentation that is continuously embellished and enhanced, and then used in whole or in parts, to express our Voice in the world. The facts and figures can be updated, but the key themes that underpin the creation and emergence of a new world, a new set of paradigms or approaches to yield a better future, remain. By focusing on our Voice, rather than the needs of each presentation one at a time, we can build a strong strategic stage presence over time. Listening to a presenter with mastery over their material and inspired by a great cause, is mesmerizing.

A Compelling Signature Presentation Expresses Our Voice

Most presentations however are not inspiring. They are linear and logical connecting the past with the present and projecting this stream of thoughts into the future. They are discursive and descriptive, reporting what has happened or is now happening without giving the data strategic context or exploring evolutionary shifts.

This means little changes. Proposals for new initiatives and investments are rooted in solving current issues rather than presenting daring and bold invitations to address the root cause. We must shift from reporting the observable to articulating what is possible. To be inspiring and strategic, our presentation needs to be set in the context of higher aspirations, paradigm shifts, big promises and visionary outcomes.

One of the things I've commonly found amongst my coaching clients, is that we rarely appreciate our Voice let alone articulate it. We don't take time to consider what we really think. Rather we simply negotiate and navigate our way through each day and in relation to each presentation opportunity. Yet when asked, my clients always know what they really think. Our views are lying just beneath our conscious reality. By bringing our thoughts front of mind, we can begin to inquire into our purpose, release our Voice and articulate it through words and pictures.

Our Views Are Lying Just Beneath Our Conscious Reality

It is essential to do this in order to empower others. If our people do not understand the strategic context we see, it is very challenging for them to make decisions that are strategically aligned. Everyone sees a different picture of the present based on their previous experiences, beliefs and expectations. We are constantly screening what we hear and only notice and pay attention to things we can connect with. We are also continuously judging what we hear in relation to what we already understand. This is why no two people describe an incident or event in the same way.

Developing and advocating a strategic perspective helps everyone in the organization and external stakeholders to appreciate how their goals, needs and concerns fit into the bigger picture. Further, by inquiring into and engaging other people's perspectives, we can develop a deeper and broader shared perspective that simultaneously enables growth and development. We learn and develop mutual understanding and trust through open, constructive, collaborative conversations.

We Develop Our Awareness Through Open Conversations

It is important to communicate iteratively. When we listen to a message, we take in elements that connect with our own experience and knowledge. When it is all new and apparently unrelated to what we already know, it takes much longer for new knowledge to take hold in the neural networks of our brain. Therefore we must address the challenge of remembering and interpreting what we present to others by getting into the minds of our audience. Acronyms can be a very useful memory jog.

Further, unless we generate a thought ourselves, it is much less likely to be well understood. Thus it also important to balance advocacy with inquiry by asking questions and providing time for our audience to form their own opinions and then expand their perspectives to take account of new information that is outside of their current experience.

Developing a Compelling Signature Presentation enables us to articulate our strategic agenda more fully, openly and convincingly. It takes us from being absent to being truly present, from being an observer to an influencer, from being a reporter to a leader. And when we make an authentic, inspiring presentation of what the future could be, we are presenting others with the gift of our unique futuristic perspective so that together we might make a greater contribution to the prosperity and wellbeing of our communities and advance our civilization.

Our Unique Perspective Is A Gift That Can Inspire Others

The expression of a Compelling Signature Presentation is the mark of the *Strategist*. The *Strategist* is committed to a future they wish to create and speaks openly and convincingly on how that future could be created. They are self-validating and therefore confident, yet open and embracing of others and therefore also compassionate. The *Strategist* speaks to a wide and diverse audience externally as well as to the people they are directly responsible for leading. An authentic, articulate Voice with an open mind and an open heart is a mark of the *Strategist*.

In contrast, as an *Achiever* we appreciate the importance of a Vision of the future that we articulate in terms of specific goals and targets over the next one to three years. Establishing a Vision begins at the *Achiever* level and is extended over longer time horizons at the *Catalyst* and *Strategist* levels. As a *Catalyst* we tune into our Values so that we appreciate when we are being true to ourselves and when we are slightly off. This enables us to inquire, understand, adjust and learn, to become more self-aware.

Then as we consolidate our congruence with higher order Values and become self-validating through the course of being true to ourselves and standing in our own power, we enter the *Strategist* stage. We learn to develop our courageous authenticity as a *Strategist* where we take accountability for blazing a new pathway to a visionary future 7+/-2 years out! In this way we bring forward the expression of our authentic Voice in the world in order to serve others.

A Compelling Signature Presentation Signals the *Strategist*

Our Voice at *Achiever* level reports the past and anticipates the future; our Voice at Catalyst level encourages participation to engage in what the future could be; and our Voice at *Strategist* exhorts and empowers others to take accountability for creating a transformational Vision of the future which leads to significantly improved mutually beneficial outcomes for all. Our Voice shifts from reporting and engaging others to advocating a particular perspective and articulating the thought-bridges and mental pictures people need to make sense of the *Strategist's* broader and deeper perspective.

The development of a Compelling Signature Presentation is based on 12 P's that inspire, influence and convince. The first set of 4 P's inspire. They start with making a big <u>Promise</u>. *Strategists* make big Promises because they can see the possible future and are committed to bringing it about. They are fervent and enthusiastic. If you are going to take people on an uncertain, potentially precipitous journey, you need to make the destination worthwhile. We can only know what we can and cannot do until we've tried and learned, and then tried some more!

This is followed through by articulating the higher order <u>Principles</u> that are at stake and incredibly important to follow. These may include social justice, equal opportunity, human compassion or environmental sustainability. We must also have a <u>Point</u> stated clearly and simply in language that is easily understood and repeatable like a motto e.g. "to breakthrough and break free". And the fourth P is to bring your presentation alive by making it <u>Personal</u> to you. How has your life experience informed your perspective? Share your emotional experience with your audience so that it becomes real to them.

Secondly it's important to influence with the facts and by igniting our imagination. The second set of P's include before and after <u>Pictures</u>; <u>Positioning</u> of our case in relation to known data, supportive or unsupportive, with relevant rationales; the <u>Paradigm</u> shifts that you are asking people to make in terms of making new trade-offs; and the <u>Proof</u> that what you are suggesting has succeeded before with proven results!

Now you have them on board and it's time to convince your audience resoundingly so that they are converted from bystanders to followers. The ninth P is <u>People</u>, the audience itself. It is essential to talk to them directly, to address their needs, motives, desires and fears. Then you can enchant and excite them with your <u>Passion</u>, your zeal and commitment to carry out your Promise. Penultimately you must make a <u>Pitch</u> – what would you like your audience to do or what decision would you like them to make? They want to help and need to know how to get involved. And finally, developing your stage <u>Presence</u> is essential. We fake it till we make it!

The 12 P's Serve to Inspire, Influence and Convince Others

I have witnessed the amazing increase in invitations to make presentations that have come to my clients once they have begun to make good steady progress in implementing the first 5 steps and begun to explore what they really think deep down. And I have also been agreeably surprised by the tremendous impression they make as outstanding speakers despite personal qualities such as shyness which would suggest otherwise. Once they have their Strategic Agenda firmly in mind and the ship has sailed so to speak, they move their audiences as a result of their authenticity and commitment. As we become adept and practiced at expressing our authentic message publicly, we begin to develop the eloquence and charisma of the *Alchemist*.

"Our deepest fear is not that we are inadequate.
Our deepest fear is that we are powerful beyond measure.
It is our light, not our darkness that most frightens us.
We ask ourselves, "Who am I to be brilliant, gorgeous, talented, fabulous?"
Actually, who are you not to be?" - **Marianne Williamson**

KEY IDEAS

1. Having a single holistic and futuristic Compelling Signature Presentation enables us to establish a strong strategic stage presence and attract followers.

2. Even if we have not articulated the fullness of our beliefs and grand visions of the future before, our views lie just beneath our conscious awareness. We can discern them through the process of inquiry.

3. The courage and confidence to articulate and engage others in our personal aspirations of the future is inspiring for all involved and leads to true collaboration and emergent solutions.

4. By building on our Compelling Signature Presentation over time, we develop confidence, mastery of our subject and grow more alert to new subtleties and insights that help to develop further understanding and foresight.

For more information on Stage Leadership Development, go to www.antoinettebraks/stages

For more information on Executive SOS, go to www.antoinettebraks/SOS

Chapter 7

Leverage SCALE

Orchestrated Stakeholder Engagement

"I alone cannot change the world, but I can cast a stone across the water to create many ripples." - Mother Teresa

Mastery of Engagement

As *Specialists*, we identify with our work, our expertise, and our professional reputation. Our work defines our identity. We feel the need to prove ourselves worthy and we do this largely through our work in terms of doing our best to produce what's required and earning an income to support ourselves and our family. We're very work oriented and rooted in parochial matters that have a direct impact on us. Our focus is narrow confining our view of the world to our immediate surroundings.

As *Achievers*, we focus on achieving results and short to medium term outcomes. We learn to become customer centric ensuring that we match our commitments with deliverables, endeavoring to under-promise and over-deliver. We perform extremely effectively in business-as-usual, performing to the required standard of service and level of customer satisfaction. We cooperate with others to achieve pragmatic results. Our identity relates to our effectiveness to turn our productivity into value for others.

As *Catalysts*, we move beyond meeting project deadlines and service deliverables, to engage directly with our customers and other stakeholders. Our focus shifts to understanding people and their experience in the world in order to forge better and more innovative solutions that address the core cause rather than just resolve the problems that arise. Building authentic rather than transactional relationships requires us to become more authentic and also to better understand others in an intrinsically supportive way. As we develop self-awareness, our hearts open up to other people's experiences and challenges, and our minds open up to collaboration and innovation.

As we gradually adopt the role of *Strategist*, we integrate our understanding of ourselves and others to co-create mutually beneficial goals and generate outcomes that serve the greater good. In this way we start to transform business operations and services with pioneering thinking and more advanced technology to better meet the needs of the whole community, both those directly involved as well as those indirectly affected. In this way we transcend current operating systems and advance society.

Thus the significance of Orchestrated Stakeholder Engagement as we progress from the *Specialist* and *Achiever* mindsets, to that of *Catalyst* and onto *Strategist*.

Gary's Story

Gary was in his early 40's. He wanted to become more strategic and to be highly effective as a leader. He was purposeful, positive and enthusiastic, and he held genuine aspirations about making a significant difference through his work.

Gary had previously been a member of the police force and had recently moved into an Executive role within Family and Community Services. It was a 3-year Contract where he was responsible for the transition of children in out-of-home-care from centralized services to localized community services provided by NGOs and NFPs.

It was a significant undertaking. There were substantial changes in processes and relationships for the many people involved, sensitivities around service costs and child welfare, and the transition needed to be completed within challenging timeframes. Many new NGOs and NFPs were needed to expand the services to be offered to the families and children in out-of-home-care. Further, there was also the risk of significant media exposure if things didn't go well.

One of Gary's most striking characteristics was his big heart. He really cared about the children and people involved in the transition. For Gary it wasn't just about making the project happen by driving hard towards deadlines. For him, the transition project was an opportunity to generate better outcomes for everyone involved.

First he articulated a new set of guiding principles: child first, family unity and carer support, to establish a framework for decision-making. The shift from centralized services to community accountability changed the roles and responsibilities of all stakeholders. It was important that communities felt empowered to make decisions aligned with government policy and universal principles.

Gary had a good sense of his role as a Catalyst rather than an Achiever. While Achievers focused on driving for results, Catalysts focus on effective engagement with the people involved so that their collaborative efforts lead to the desired results. Relationships come first. While Achievers could rely on positional authority, Catalysts need to develop personal authenticity to attract support and influence others to lead to the mutual achievement of shared outcomes.

Gary developed an overarching strategic framework that would embrace all interested parties. He set up an iterative engagement process so that all parties could come together in small groups to talk through their approach and the timelines for implementation. He also conducted a series of large forums or summits that brought many people together to finalize a concerted approach for each community.

These various engagement strategies together constituted a campaign. It was brought together by the theme: "It takes a community to raise a child." In his opening presentation Gary wore his heart on his sleeve stepping into his role as a genuinely authentic leader. He created a community-centric business model outlining the different roles to be played by different members of the community and government. He finished his presentation with the following words:

> "I'm here to make a difference,
> To give kids a good start.
> To bring people together
> With Hope, Faith and Heart.

Hope for a brighter future
Faith that we can do it
And our Hearts full of love."

His campaign to engage and initiate a collaborative effort was so successful that the community service providers started to help each other. The more experienced NGOs and NFPs helped the new organizations set up the required systems and processes to ensure effective implementation. They also worked together to optimize the results for each child being placed in out-of-home-care. Rather than compete or move to the first solution, they collaborated on multiple decisions simultaneously, in the best interests of all the children and families involved.

Gary took his engagement circle wider by including health and education service providers to advance the children's wellbeing. The serious challenge to respond adequately and effectively to child abuse reports required everyone to play an integral and proactive part in the safety, health and wellbeing of each child.

Gary described his growth as follows:

> *"My defensiveness has dropped. I'm changing my thinking, creating my own identity. I'm my own person now. People are coming to me to ask questions, which I can confidently answer. People are also picking up the phone with their problems."*

When the transition of services from the government to the community was well underway, a new set of Regional Director roles were established. They were responsible for integrating all social services within the region including out-of-home-care for children as well as support services for the disabled, elderly and homeless. Gary was the only new person who was appointed to a Regional role from his organization. He was recognized as someone who engaged proactively and widely, someone who could bring people together to build vibrant, healthy communities.

Since that time Gary has been taking the initiative to lead his division of 1000+ people and build their brand around a shared set of values. He has established a one-stop-shop for all the community's social support services where each service representative is familiar with all their services and can therefore take a child and family-centric approach. And just recently, he launched his new regional campaign where 300 NGOs and 110 NFPs came together to explore aspirational community outcomes to create social wellbeing and how they were going to achieve this. He is highly regarded as a pioneer in his industry.

Gary said:

> *"I'm always looking for the next part of my life … being satisfied is the wrong word … I am fulfilled and content … I'm happy yet always looking for something else. I've let go of my old identity, achieving, being impatient. I no longer need to be focused, but to be open to do whatever is required, not because you need to do it but because the universe asks it of you. I know that good will come from any and every situation. I'm allowing the joy of life to be a part of my life. Now I'm quite free!"*

ORCHESTRATED STAKEHOLDER ENGAGEMENT

"If you want to make peace with your enemy, you have to work with your enemy. Then he becomes your partner."
- Nelson Mandela

In our achievement driven world where time is of the essence and it's important to get more and more done, most Stakeholder Engagement takes place during the implementation phase of projects. If they are lucky, stakeholders are consulted on what is probably going to be happening when and invited to comment. However mostly they are told and invited to ask questions in relation to implementation. This very limited form of engagement, akin to master-servant, is something we've become accustomed to. It creates compliance which is one of the reasons 40% of the Executive population remain anchored in the mindset of a *Conformist*.

When implementation is driven through an organization and the opportunity for engagement is limited to feedback and questions to get more information, we are forcing and compelling others rather than engaging and collaborating with them. We are doing things to people, imposing new criteria, processes or situations on them, rather than enabling them to participate actively in those decisions.

As customers we're often also limited in our engagement. We're asked for our feedback on specific incidents or events, or in relation to specific services and situations. However these generally limit our contribution to evaluating specific questions and services on a scale from bad to excellent. They tend not to reinvent or re-engineer the offering. Feedback is quite different from input. When input is requested, most make suggestions that relate to the event or service itself leading to more fundamental changes in the composition of the service or product offering.

Asking For Input Is Much More Engaging Than Feedback

Further, feedback in and of itself is a manifestation of our own mindset. If we are a positive encouraging person like the *Achiever*, then we will offer this type of feedback. If we are a naysayer below this level, we will offer negative feedback. *Conformists* are renown for making complaints. When they are compliant they give their power away and they attempt to redress this balance by making complaints about others. Thus feedback is more of a projection of the participant's worldview than necessarily a robust evaluation of a particular product or performance.

To engage authentically with another person is to invite them to voice their views. Thus the common connection of Voice in Steps 6 and 7. In Step 6 we master our own Voice, and in Step 7, we master how to actively engage the Voice of others. We do this by engaging proactively prior to any solution being devised. And we do this genuinely by being open to the form that solution will take. Then we continue to engage by reviewing proposed solutions and inviting people affected to comment, contribute and change the nature of the proposed solution. Doing this in a systematic way while bringing various stakeholders together from time to time builds a genuine sense of community.

Workshops are a primary form of engagement today. They involve open questions so that people can genuinely contribute their ideas, concerns, fears and deepest desires. Workshops can also go beyond engaging on the problem, to exploring the underlying issues from many different viewpoints. The use of workshops as sounding boards to build mutual understanding is a very valuable use of time. They are a great way to generate increased self-awareness as it's often the only time our point of view is actively sought out amidst listening to others' perspectives in a situation where multiple stakeholders are brought together. When a group is asked to form proposals, they must also seek to bridge the gaps and disconnects amongst diverse views.

Multi-Stakeholder Forums Increase Mutual Awareness

The *Conformist*, *Specialist* and *Achiever* mentalities that prevail in organizations, inhibit engagement. Their focus is on the task, the work and the result, rather than the relationship. They seek to do, not to understand. Whereas engagement is the number one priority for the *Catalyst*. Simply by including genuine engaging events in your organization's Calendar, you will be encouraging Stage Leadership Development. The Cascading Team Charter and fortnightly cycle of Strategic and Culture meetings will do much to engage the people inside your organization, and the shared articulation of a series of Values can also be extended to the external community of stakeholders.

Engagement with your direct reports and management team

can also be enhanced in a number of other ways. Typically most Executives ask their people to propose new initiatives or projects to increase efficiency, enhance effectiveness or uplift performance in some way. Their Managers then put something together for them, often on their own without consulting their own team. This document is then "corrected" by you, the Executive, to better reflect your ideas and intentions. This process continues back and forth until the proposal is agreed and then put forward for approval by others.

This approach involves a lot of duplication in redoing the same piece of work many times over and it is also disempowering. First, it consumes time and makes the person creating the document feel like they're not able to get it right – indeed, they keep getting it wrong! If they are operating at *Specialist*, they will be identifying with their work and will take this feedback personally. This leads to lower self-esteem and inhibits their growth. After a while they will no longer give the document a lot of thought as their expectation will be that you will amend it anyway so it's just not worth their investment of time. Thus the secondary impact, disengagement and lessened accountability.

Orchestrated Stakeholder Engagement involves open, collaborative engagement with the people directly concerned in the proposal, project or initiative, whether inside or outside the organization. It invokes roles of Sponsor and Champion requiring collaborative effort rather then the separate individual efforts of Manager and Subordinate where approval is sought. This ensures that participation is voluntary and vibrant and that the responsibility to take the initiative and drive new initiatives forward is held at the appropriate level. This process creates a stream of engagement rather than a series of roadblocks.

Shift From Correcting Work to Sponsoring Initiatives

A second dimension of the process concerns the development of a prototype or Strawman. The prototype is tested by user groups, while the Strawman is pulled apart and put back together by interest groups. Their opportunity to be involved in this way invites active participation leading to significant levels of engagement. This is quite distinctive from a "buy-in" process where proposed new initiatives are shared widely and comments are sought.

Genuine engagement requires a process of inquiry, not just feedback. Once the inquiry process has taken place – the appreciative inquiry process SOAR (Strengths, Opportunities, Aspirations and Results) is a great place to start – only then can any new product, proposed solution or strategic agenda be promoted or documented more widely for final comments and views. At this time the people who have been actively involved in creating the solution will own and defend it.

Real Engagement Puts Inquiry and Listening Before Input

I call this type of engagement being in the orange light zone of the *Catalyst*. The *Conformist* and *Specialist* are largely concerned with red lights. This is what they're on the lookout for – when not to proceed, when to stop, when to be passive or otherwise be at risk for getting something wrong. The *Achiever* looks for green lights. They want to know when to proceed and get going. They're keen to move forward and learn, adjust and refine, and keep on producing useful results for others.

The *Catalyst* as I said prefers the orange light zone. In the orange light zone we can do what we like. We can stop or go. We do not need to ask permission – wait for green – or stop unless we choose to. Rather we proceed with care, engaging, engaging and engaging, to gradually build momentum towards an optimized solution. You will not find a person operating at

Catalyst ever asking for permission and you will find them doing innovative things, taking risks, where they have not been given approval or even communicated their intentions to anyone. They're moving in flow.

This becomes a problem for conventional organizations because they are not built around engagement processes. They are built around risk management and bureaucratic approval processes. However better for the organization to adopt this Strategic Operating System and provide for regular channels of engagement that open the doorways for increased authentic communications, than to shut down the evolving *Catalyst*. To do so is to inhibit the growth and evolution of their organization and business. Sadly the reverse happens more often as most conventional organizations are still run by *Achievers* and view any unapproved conduct that the *Catalyst* initiates as radical and inappropriate.

The Orange Light Zone Brings the *Catalyst* Alive

Once the *Catalyst* has been allowed to roam free rather than be reined in, their experimental approaches to innovate and collaborate with others, leads to greater self-awareness of their purpose and their intrinsic power. As they start to experience the support of others and the manifestation of serendipitous events, they become emboldened. Over the course of time they learn to exercise courageous authenticity in the face of challenges to their integrity, and then become the green light as a *Strategist*. A *Strategist* is self-validating and will naturally lean into a position where they will wield the personal authority or thought leadership and hold the positional authority or followership, to set direction and provide guidance.

The *Strategist's* appreciation of self amidst multiple perspectives grows only through roles that engage wide internal stakeholders or external stakeholders. Thus typical *Catalyst* roles in organizations are business partner roles for functional divisions – provided they are not only responsible for implementation but also for strategic engagement; and marketing roles within business divisions that interface with customers and clients at a strategic level. By strategic in this context I mean being involved in the creation of the future rather than just the delivery against current commitments. *Catalysts* also often hold strategic consulting roles.

Catalysts Thrive in Roles That Demand Wide Engagement

A third element of Stakeholder Engagement is building relationships. Much of relationship building within and across organizations today is transactional. It's akin to: must have a coffee with X because they may of help to me one day and need to stay on their good side. Or: must have a drink with Y because they've just got a promotion and will now have the ear of one of my key customers. This type of relationship building is largely based on "you scratch my back and I'll scratch yours." Favors are expected to be reciprocated. This is the game of politics where loyalty has been known to out-manoeuver ethics.

In contrast, transformational relationship building takes place in the context of a Strategic Agenda focused on mutual community interest rather than self-interest. It includes a Stakeholder Map, a Relationship Index to measure the current nature of the relationship and the desired relationship leading to goal setting, and an Account Management or Business Partnership Framework that establishes accountabilities for goal achievement. By placing an *Achiever's* framework around Stakeholder Engagement, *Achiever's* shift a little more comfortably to the next stage of *Catalyst*.

Stakeholders are defined by whether or not they have a stake in the future Vision, either as actors, receivers or observers. Orchestrated Stakeholder Engagement encompasses active engagement with key stakeholders to develop an understanding of their perspectives and seek to learn from them and influence them. The development of the relationship is an outcome in and of itself – and often a Strategic Shift in Culture that is essential to build bridges before the work of developing new transformational solutions can even begin.

Building Partnerships Is A Strategic Culture Shift

The nature of Stakeholder Engagement is to explore and better understand the needs, desires, concerns and aspirations of all who will be implicated in creating the future. Mutual understanding is essential to build an accord. Stakeholder Engagement is thereby a process that deepens over time as trust is built through the expression and acceptance of voluntary and vulnerable Voices. By utilizing the Dynamic Diary Rhythm to create an appropriate pattern of conscious engagement, akin to a campaign, we can foster the development of mutual awareness, increased attention and the practice of higher intentions to generate sustainable community outcomes that benefit all.

Holding a diversity of perspectives in heart and mind is a hallmark of the *Strategist*. It becomes possible through the process of deepening self-awareness of our life experience and our self-expression leading to the development of compassion for self, and the dedicated intention to better understand and genuinely care for others. This is in contrast to the more usual convention to argue or debate with others. In genuine engagement, heart rules the head. The heart listens at a deeper level to understand and empathize with the other person's experience.

We can design Orchestrated Stakeholder Engagement through an agreed Calendar of Events to engage diverse stakeholders with clear intention and conscious attention. By engaging them in your Transformational Strategic Agenda you will be able to exercise inspiring, strategic and collaborative leadership from the front as well as in ancillary conversations to listen to and understand their unique perspectives. The art of open inquiry, active listening and open conversations in the emergent future blossom through the course of Orchestrated Stakeholder Engagement.

Mutual Respect Leads to Stronger Community Outcomes

"I am of the opinion that my life belongs to the whole community and as I live, it is my privilege to do for it whatever I can. I want to be thoroughly used up when I die, for the harder I work, the more I love. I rejoice in life for it's own sake. Life is no brief candle to me; it is a sort of splendid torch which I've got hold of for the moment and I want to make it burn as brightly as possible before handing it onto future generations."
- George Bernard Shaw

KEY IDEAS

1. Proactive Stakeholder Engagement seeking input rather than feedback enables authentic engagement rather than transactional 'buy-in' giving people the opportunity to express their Voices and to be heard.

2. Open workshops which provide the opportunity for multiple stakeholder inquiry and engagement where everyone is able to develop their point of view while listening to diverse perspectives, builds mutual understanding and ownership of emergent solutions.

3. The incorporation of open engagement processes on strategic concerns for both employees and stakeholders facilitates Stage Leadership Development and the opportunity to renew organizational goals, generate new opportunities and realize aspirational outcomes.

4. Developing stakeholder relationships to build mutual understanding and increase group awareness of the strategic context generates a heightened sense of trust and strengthens community identity that is a valuable goal in and of itself to lead to transcendent solutions in the future.

For more information on Stage Leadership Development, go to www.antoinettebraks/stages

For more information on Executive SOS, go to www.antoinettebraks/SOS

NEXT STEPS

EXECUTIVE

If you would like to take the next important steps to establishing your own Strategic Operating System then please go to www.antoinettebraks.com/SOS and register for a free series of training videos so that you can get started.

I'll show you how to set up Executive Management Team Meetings in your Dynamic Diary Rhythm; how to launch your Transformational Strategic Agenda with an enlightening Purpose Statement and Strategic Shifts; and how to leverage the use of Cascading Team Charters so that you bring the whole organization together onto the same song sheet!

Take the opportunity to become an inspiring strategic leader today so that you too can join the elite 10% of Executive leaders who are *Catalysts* within 12 months knowing that you will gradually evolve to develop the capacity of a *Strategist*, the rare 5% of executive leaders who are able to transform our world.

In so doing you will unlock your creativity, double your productivity, empower your people, engage your stakeholders, lift your profile and achieve breakthrough results!

Enjoy your transformational journey to realize your purpose and your potential to lead a meaningful and fulfilling life.

All the best,
Antoinette

*"The higher our self-expression and the deeper our self-awareness,
the richer our life experience and the greater our soul evolution."*
- Antoinette Braks

For more information on Stage Leadership Development, go to www.antoinettebraks/stages

For more information on Executive SOS, go to www.antoinettebraks/SOS

ACKNOWLEDGEMENTS

I would like to extend my heartfelt appreciation to my coaching clients, especially Jane, Richard, Greg, Kate, Jason, John and Gary who kindly allowed me to tell their stories of revelation and accomplishment during the course of our coaching collaboration. It's due to their courage, discipline and aspirational intent that the 7-Step Program was distilled and refined.

I would also like to thank Christine Broad, Senior Consultant at Hudson Talent Management Sydney Australia for her support and kindness as we collaborated to establish my coaching practice there following the SES Development Centre for the NSW Public Sector.

I also very much appreciate the guidance and support of Maxine Whitlock who has read and offered advice on many early versions of this book, and the artistry and attentiveness of Lucy Deslandes, creator of my book cover.

Thank you all!

ABOUT THE AUTHOR

Antoinette Braks

Recently Antoinette has worked as an Executive Coach in Strategic Leadership for 50+ Senior Executives. A group of her clients participated in her Doctoral Research Study. It was found that each Executive moved a full stage, most to *Catalyst* (making up just 10% of Executive Leaders) and one to *Strategist* (a rare 5%) with a second knocking on its door.

These results are considered remarkable as previously it was thought that Stage Development generally took place over a two-three year period of committed focus to personal development. However, as a result of her coaching program in Strategic and Holistic Leadership, her clients each progressed a full stage without exception, advancing their careers and producing outstanding results for their organizations.

The 7-Step Strategic Operating System is a distillation of the strategic scaffolding Antoinette guided her clients to build in order to establish a strong and secure platform for their progression as *Catalysts* and *Strategists*. It is available online as STRATEGIC IGNITION.

Go to www.antoinettebraks.com/SOS to find out more about this proven online program in Stage Leadership Development from *Achiever* to *Catalyst* and onto *Strategist*.

Career Highlights

In her career Antoinette has specialized in Holistic Leadership and Organizational Development, empowering People and Culture frameworks and setting Aspirational Strategic Direction alongside Scorecard Governance and building a Values Culture.

She has led the Organizational Transformation of a 1,000-person business services organization where People Engagement shifted by a quantum leap of 30% within six months of launch. In another instance her empowering people leadership and management frameworks enabled a small trading company to more than double its revenues within three weeks of their implementation.

Antoinette is highly versed in the strategic facilitation of Aspirational Strategic Off-Sites for Senior Executive Teams across multiple industry and government sectors.

She has also worked as a leading Management Assessment Consultant having conducted over 500 assessments of Senior Executives in the public sector with Hudson Talent Management and through the course of regional succession planning and merger and acquisition assignments with Top 50 corporations in Asia Pacific with Korn Ferry International.

She has led People and Culture Policy across Latin America and Africa for Shell International and was the General Manager People and Culture for Vector, energy infrastructure company in New Zealand.

Early in her career she became the top performer in Executive Selection and Search with Australasian market leader, Morgan & Banks.

Education

Her education includes a PhD (c) at the Macquarie Graduate School of Management (MGSM), an MA in Management Research (MGSM), MBA at London Business School, LLB (Hons) and BA (Political Science) at Auckland University and Dip Intl Mktg (Hons). She has been awarded two University prizes for Excellence by the Macquarie Graduate School of Management.

"The higher our self-expression and the deeper our self-awareness, the richer our life experience and the greater our soul evolution."
- Antoinette Braks

For more information on Stage Leadership Development, go to www.antoinettebraks/stages

For more information on Executive SOS, go to www.antoinettebraks/SOS

Made in the USA
Middletown, DE
27 September 2023

39482209R00096